SECRET
LIVERPOOL
AN UNUSUAL GUIDE

Mike Keating

JONGLEZ PUBLISHING

travel guides

Born and educated in Liverpool, **Mike Keating** continues to live in the city centre, where he maintains a keen interest in the local heritage and its history. He is a retired university lecturer and writer with a short acting and directing career at the Unity Theatre and an even shorter one as a cartoonist on the *Liverpool Echo*. This is his first guide-book which also marks his debut in the world of photographic illustration.

Liverpool is a city of secret places, quirky artefacts and objects with a hidden story to tell. *Secret Liverpool - An unusual guide* is a journey of discovery through these hidden corners and urban myths. Through its pages, we discover that things are not what they appear to be: objects and places we take for granted in our everyday lives reveal the surprising stories that shaped Liverpool's shoreline, streetscape and skyline and the lives of its people.

Intended as a pocket guide for the keen city stroller (Liverpool has been voted one of 'the World's Most Walkable Cities'), *Secret Liverpool - An unusual guide* can also be used by those who prefer to tour by bike (www.citybikeliverpool. co.uk) or enjoyed by those who would rather travel no further than their armchair.

It also draws attention to the multitude of details found in places that we may pass every day without noticing. We invite you to look more closely at the urban landscape and to see your own city with the curiosity and attention that we often display while travelling elsewhere ...

You can't surprise all of the people all of the time but this unusual guide should have enough surprises to keep everyone on their toes. We hope you get as much pleasure out of it as we did compiling it.

Comments on this guidebook and its contents, as well as information on places we may not have mentioned, are more than welcome and will enrich future editions.
Don't hesitate to contact us:
E-mail: info@jonglezpublishing.com
Jonglez Publishing
25 rue du Maréchal Foch
78000 Versailles, France

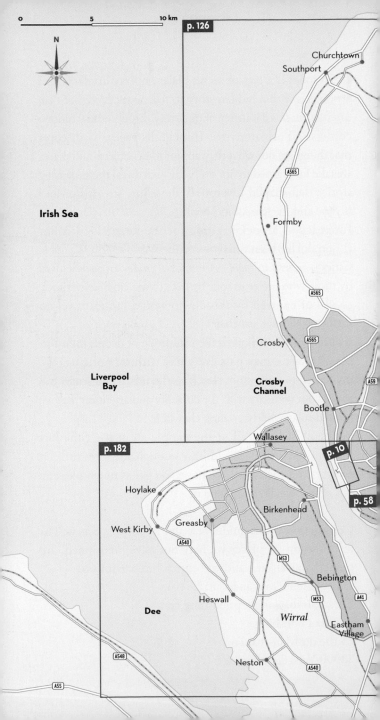

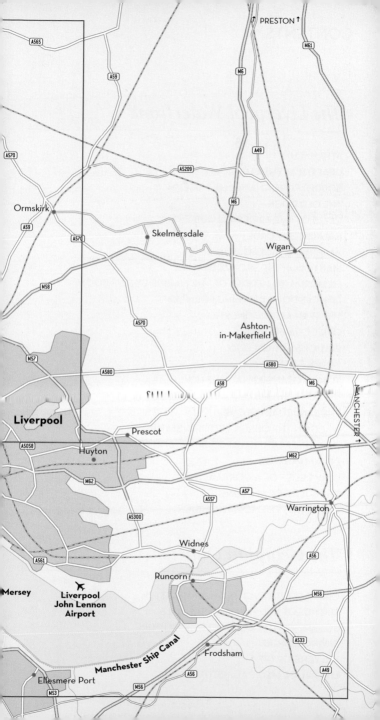

CONTENTS

The Liverpool Waterfront

The Georgian Quarter

The Northend / Southport

CONTENTS

The Southend / Wirral

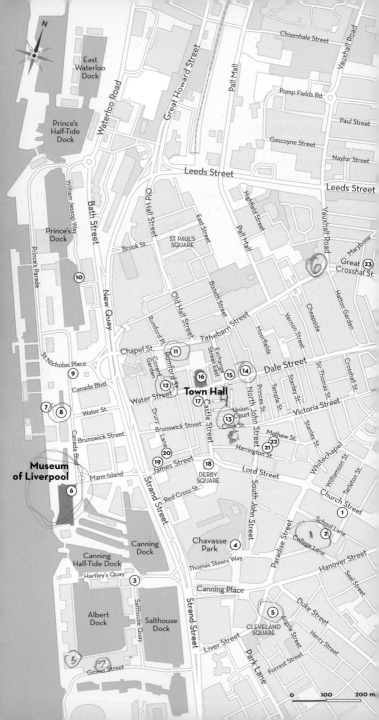

The Liverpool Waterfront

World Museum
+ Walker Art Gallery
fossils p. 117
see p. 213

1. bluecoat display, bluecoat garden
2. Fab4 - shop/cafe
3. The Nest - shop
4. Magic Willow - shop - 8 Mathew Street
5. Eleanor Rigsby statue
6. Superlamb banana

ATHENAEUM

Liverpool's great literary resource

Church Alley, L1 3DD
0151 709 7770
www.theathenaeum.org.uk
Guided tours operate weekly and can be booked online
Also open during Heritage Open Days
Central station or Liverpool One bus station

ounded as a gentlemen's club in 1797 – despite being named after a
Greek goddess – the Athenaeum was originally located on Church
Street but moved to this side street in 1928, where its existence is known
to few but the membership (aka Proprietors).

At a time when Liverpool was fast becoming the nation's second
port and had a burgeoning middle class of merchants, professionals and
clerics, the need for a reading room with a regular supply of newspapers,
periodicals and commercial pamphlets was keenly felt by gentlemen
of trade who did not relish the coffee house as a place to take in the
important events of the day. The original building opened in 1800 next to
St Peter's Pro-Cathedral on Church Street, the town's main thoroughfare.

In 1924, the council demolished both buildings to widen the road

(no surprise there), the church making way for the first Woolworth's store in Britain. A small brass crucifix in the pavement outside Liverpool ONE marks the position of the altar (see page 181). By all accounts (well, one actually), St Peter's was no architectural beauty, but the Athenaeum was a different matter and the Committee insisted on a move to a new build on the site of St Peter's cemetery around the corner, where its original interior inspired the decor.

The library contains over 60,000 books, drawings and maps, including the personal collection of William Roscoe. Bankrupted in 1815, he was forced to sell his beloved library, so members clubbed together and bought the lot, which they donated to the Athenaeum for his continued use.

Also on show are Liverpool's handwritten census from 1801, a copy of the Magna Carta, Henry VIII's *Defence of the Seven Sacraments* and a *Pyrotechnia* from 1611 for any budding terrorist well-versed in Latin. The secret ballot box for the election of members has survived from 1797 and is still in use today. The expression 'blackballed' stems from the use of such ballots: one black ball in the 'No' compartment and you were barred. Amazing they had any members at all given that early Proprietors were both slavers and abolitionists. Women were finally admitted in 1995 but still need to go through the process.

GRAFFITI AT THE BLUECOAT

The UK's earliest arts centre

School Lane, L1 3BX
www.thebluecoat.org.uk
9am–6pm
Central station or Liverpool One bus station

One of Liverpool's oldest and best-loved buildings, the Bluecoat retains several features that date back some three centuries. It has 70,000 visitors a year but how many stop to admire the oldest graffiti in

Liverpool? Hidden for years, renovation work in 2005–2008 revealed dates and initials etched into the cornerstone of the building to the right of the courtyard. Most likely culprits? Bored schoolkids for whom this was an 18th-century playground.

Also easy to miss, perched above the doorway of Kernaghan's bookshop (well worth a browse!), is the city's longest-serving Liver Bird. Carved in stone, it dates from the 1700s and should not be confused with the cast-iron version opposite, added some 100 years later.

Founded in 1708 by slave trader Bryan Blundell and his chum, the Rev. Robert Styth, the original Blue Coat Hospital was replaced in 1717 by the present building to provide boarding accommodation for children from poor backgrounds in the new Parish of Liverpool. The boarders spent two-thirds of the day at work (making stockings and pins and picking oakum). The school even sold their urine to the wool trade as a softener. The back courtyard (aka 'Liverpool's secret oasis') was the Master's Garden around which almshouses were built. In the 19th century, they were replaced by school workshops, now home to mixed-use creative tenancies. In the 1770s, the school abolished child labour and introduced music and the arts into the curriculum (the kids thanked the enlightened governors with a mass breakout).

When the school moved to Wavertree in 1906, the building became home to rebel artists from the university's Art Sheds. Refusing to join the newly opened College of Art, the Sandon Studios camped out in what is now the Liverpool Institute for Performing Arts car park and then moved into the Bluecoat Hospital building. An exhibition of Monet in 1908 and Post-Impressionists in 1911 (the first time the likes of Matisse, Gauguin and Picasso had been seen outside London) established it as the earliest arts centre in the country. Its tenure was secured when Fanny Lister (later Calder) set up the Bluecoat Society of Arts in 1925 for those 'interested in something more than fashion and football and bridge and the share market'.

Over the years, the Bluecoat has played host to the UK's oldest film society, Jacob Epstein's controversial sculpture *Genesis,* Yoko Ono's first-ever paid performance (involving a broom, two ladders and a vase) and the first exhibition of Captain Beefheart's paintings. Bartok, Holst and Stravinsky have all paid visits while Simon Rattle attended music classes here as a kid. As home to over 30 creative designers, it continues life as a 'mixed creative centre' as well as offering respite from the daily grind that is Liverpool ONE.

The Bluecoat survived the Blitz and two moves to demolish it – the second being for a planned ring road to celebrate Liverpool's claim to be 'The City of Change and Challenge' (ho-hum!).

BORDER FORCE NATIONAL MUSEUM

The only museum of its kind in Britain

Albert Dock, L3 4AQ
www.liverpoolmuseums.org.uk/maritime/visit/floor-plan/seized
Daily, 10am–5pm
James Street station or Liverpool One bus station

In a former bonded warehouse beneath the Maritime Museum is a unique partnership between National Museums Liverpool, the UK Border Force and HMRC, devoted to the secret world of smuggling, tax fraud and border security.

A 300-year backdrop charts the history of taxation, from funding warfare to welfare (and the odd museum). On a personal level, attempts to avoid tax and import duties may be dismissed as victimless misdemeanours but turn out to be a serious threat to social cohesion and a magnet for professional criminals. The exhibition has its fair share of ingenious and amusing devices for the concealment of contraband (false legs, hollowed-out carvings and knickers big enough to hide 6kg of cocaine) but also raises awareness of organised crime and its links to drug smuggling, counterfeit goods, people trafficking and the plight of endangered species. The consequences are mind-boggling: the illicit trade in drugs, booze and fags (25% of cigarettes smoked in the UK are smuggled and half of these are fake) amounts to over £13b a year.

According to the exhibition, we lose more in tax fraud and evasion than we spend on our children's education. The recent 20% rise in gun and knife crime is largely fuelled by illegally imported weapons orchestrated by a network of veteran organised criminals ... of which Liverpool is one of the regional hubs. Poaching animals for their hides, horns and body parts has pushed some species to the brink of extinction.

Acting as a mirror to this litany of deception is a counter-display of equally ingenious measures for detection: a 6-ft wall gun used by an 18th-century border patrol, a 19th-century saccharometer, DNA-testing equipment and some of the latest interception vessels in the world. Among the paraphernalia of detection, the one that stands out is based on trust: tasked in the 19th century with containing contagious diseases, revenue officers would pass a copy of a quarantine bible to the captain of an approaching vessel upon which he was bound to swear an oath that his ship was clean. Breaches of trust incurred hefty fines or imprisonment.

A simulator allows you to command a customs cutter mission, plan for the voyage and execute an interception on the high seas.

THE OLD DOCK

'Its like is not to be seen anywhere in England'

Merseyside Maritime Museum, Albert Dock, L3 4AQ
www.liverpoolmuseums.org.uk/maritime/visit/old_dock_tours.aspx
Free tours Mon, Tues & Wed 10.30am, 12 noon and 2.30pm
5-min walk from Liverpool ONE or James Street station

Next time you need a break from shopping in Liverpool ONE, take a breather behind John Lewis and peer through the circular panel of toughened glass which marks the Old Dock. Rediscovered during the excavations for Liverpool ONE, the catalyst for Liverpool's fortune – and for the city which stretches all around you – has its very origins beneath your feet. Quite simply, without this hole in the ground Liverpool would never have emerged as a 'global gateway to the Empire'.

As late as 1660, according to local historian Mike Royden (http://www. roydenhistory.co.uk), there were only around 190 houses within the seven streets of the original town. A small coastal port and fishing town with a mud-wall fort, Liverpool lagged behind London, Bristol and Chester as a serious trade hub. Perfectly placed but on a fiercely tidal river, the port could not cope with the shipping which sought to use it. The creek, after which the Pool derived its name, was shielded from the river but depended

on the vagaries of the ebb tide to unload cargo vessels; turnaround for a decent-sized ship could take two days. In 1708, Liverpool Corporation gambled on the creation of the world's first commercial 'wet dock' and engaged a canal engineer, Thomas Steers, to construct it.

The city mortgaged itself to 'a gent in London' for £12,000 and by 1715, at twice the estimated cost, had a brick-built, gated dock on a commercial quayside (aka 'Nova Scotia') which could turn ships around in a matter of hours. The gamble paid off and sparked a massive hike in trade, particularly tobacco and sugar from the Americas and 'the blood of Africans' from the third corner in the triangular trade. Even after the abolition of the slave trade in 1807, the city continued to profit from third-party slave runners and the trade in slave goods well into the 19th century.

As 'the Western Gateway' and 'second port of the Empire', Liverpool could not help but make money; more docks were built, especially under the watchful eye of Jesse Hartley, who designed and built almost all the city's docks. But the Old Dock became a victim of its own success: it couldn't handle the demand and was made redundant by the expansion of the port. It then became an open sewer before being covered over in 1828.

Preserved by the gallons of human excrement sealing the dock, the coping stones, brickwork and wooden fender posts were unearthed during excavations in 2001. A massive archaeological dig followed in which an army of students armed with toothbrushes restored the brickwork to its original state. At the insistence of the developers, Grosvenor, the dock was incorporated into the infrastructure of Liverpool ONE, with public access retained for 1/20th of the 1.4-hectare site and daily tours available. In one corner it's possible to see the entrance to a 'sally port', an escape route from the castle which predated the dock by 500 years.

Scousers who are proud of their heritage, always tell you to 'look up' in order to appreciate the city's architecture but sometimes it's worth looking down to discover your history. The tour is free; it should be compulsory.

CELLS OF THE BRIDEWELL PUB

A bar behind bars

1 Campbell Square, Argyle Street, L1 5FB
Weekdays and Sat 12 noon–12 midnight, Sun 12 noon–9pm
Liverpool One bus station or Central station

If you must get yourself banged up on a night out in Liverpool, insist on a cell in the Ropewalks' only surviving police station. Now operating as a pub, this 19th-century cop shop can squeeze eight jailbirds into a booth behind original steel doors and barred windows.

The constables at the Campbell Square Bridewell (built in 1861) were given the impossible task of policing the toughest part of the most crime-ridden city in the UK. Their only assistance was a truncheon and 'the nightly bucket of Guinness for the Bridewell Patrol, freshly supplied from the Guinness Boats tied up in the nearby Salthouse Dock'.

No wonder that Dickens, social explorer and insomniac, was attracted to Liverpool for a closer look at the antics of the Victorian underclass and those paid to keep them in check (26,226 arrests in 1863 alone). In preparation for *The Uncommercial Traveller*, Dickens got himself sworn in as a special constable and spent the night patrolling the low spots of his second favourite city. The following extract examines the 'various unlawful traps which are every night set for (Poor Mercantile) Jack': 'There was British Jack, a little maudlin and sleepy, lolling over his empty glass, as if he were trying to read his fortune at the bottom; there was Loafing Jack of the Stars and Stripes, rather an unpromising customer, with his long nose, lank cheek, high cheek-bones, and nothing soft about him but his cabbage-leaf hat; there was Spanish Jack, with curls of black hair, rings in his ears, and a knife not far from his hand, if you got into trouble with him; there were Maltese Jack, and Jack of Sweden, and Jack the Finn, looming through the smoke of their pipes, and turning faces that looked as if they were carved out of dark wood, towards the young lady dancing the hornpipe.'

The original Toxteth riots

During the race riots of 1919 and on the day that a local black man, Charles Wooton, was hounded to his death in the King's Dock by a white mob, the Quarless family recall being housed by the Campbell Square Bridewell for their own safety. It is also claimed that the Bridewell became a detainment centre for conscientious objectors during the Second World War (unlikely) and was used as a practice space in the 1980s by local bands such as Frankie Goes to Hollywood (more likely).

What the Dickens?

While Dickens is recorded as having spent a night as a Special, the plaque proclaiming the Bridewell as the location doesn't quite add up: Sharples gives the Bridewell's completion date as 1861 but Dickens was already serialising *The Uncommercial Traveller* by 1860. So unless he was billeted on a building site, the legend is probably no more than that.

GALKOFF'S FAÇADE

The secret life of Pembroke Place

The People's Republic Gallery, Museum of Liverpool, Pier Head, Liverpool
Waterfront, L3 1DG
0151 478 4545
www.liverpoolmuseums.org.uk/mol/galkoff/

For over 80 years, Percy Galkoff's shopfront was a Pembroke Place landmark but wander along today and the listed tile work is no longer there. To track it down and immerse yourself in the history of this part of Liverpool, you must visit the top floor of the Museum of Liverpool, where the 'Secret Life of Pembroke Place' exhibition is a wonderful reconstruction of this diverse community from memories, artefacts and Galkoff's iconic tile work.

This had been the city's Jewish quarter long before the term got hijacked by smart-arse developers keen to repackage the city as something it never was – any fool knows that the whole can be comprised of no more than four quarters but Liverpool currently has ten of them!

Back in the early 20th century, this was where Jewish immigrants set up shop and reared families. As ever, the kosher butcher's shop was an essential part of the community and Galkoff's was special. Percy had it tiled in the 1930s, possibly by the local Italian craftsmen responsible for much of Liverpool's terrazzo work (they did such a good job that it was almost impossible to remove the tiles for the exhibition).

As the Jewish community started to move out post-war, the shop closed and the area fell into decline. The land was purchased by the Liverpool

School of Tropical Medicine but, confronted with a listed shopfront, they submitted a joint bid with National Museums Liverpool to the Lottery Heritage Fund. This resulted in a conservation scheme to transfer the tiles to the museum and a research project into the history of the surrounding area.

A trawl through secondary sources (newspapers, directories, etc.) created a contextual portrait of the area, with the gaps filled in by primary research into the recollections of local residents. In order to engage with the 'secret world of Pembroke Place', graphic artist Sophie Herxheimer used live sketches to record the memories of local people. As curator Poppy Learman explains, 'The technique originated as a method of engagement but it has grown legs and become the visual identity of the project.'

A thriving business area, Pembroke Place also boasted a private zoo and a roller-skating rink. Known as 'Little Hell', it had a bad reputation for crime, including several murders and the last duel fought in Liverpool.

Galkoff? He was a nice man! I worked with him.

HENRY, LIVERPOOL

All that remains of Galkoff's original site is a dilapidated block in the middle of which stand the remains of Liverpool's last surviving example of court housing: an interesting, if depressing relic crumbling away behind locked gates.

AMAZING GRACE SCULPTURE

'God moves in mysterious ways'

Pier Head Ferry Terminal Building, Georges Parade, L3 1DP
James Street station or Liverpool One bus station

The ferry terminal at the Pier Head is a strange place to discover a memorial to a slave trader, but on the staircase is a sculpture inspired by a famous hymn and clearly representing the Atlantic divided into the three elements of the triangular trade. The artist, Stephen Broadbent, studied under shipyard sculptor Arthur Dooley before establishing his own workshop at the Bridewell Studios (see page 122).

Among Broadbent's early works are the *Reconciliation* sculptures, erected in Liverpool, Glasgow and Belfast in 1989 as a 'powerful symbol of the way in which sectarianism can be overcome through the solidarity and youth of these three great cities on the Irish Sea'. Twenty years later, a similar *Reconciliation Triangle* of sculptures linked Liverpool to Cotonou in Benin and Richmond, Virginia to symbolise the slave trade connections of all three cities. The Liverpool bronze can be seen at the junction of Bold Street and Concert Square but the one we are concerned with tells a different chapter of the same story.

Commissioned for the new Mersey Ferry Terminal at the Pier Head in 2009, *Amazing Grace* has the famous lyrics etched in glass and steel. They are by John Newton, a Liverpool slaver who underwent a conversion and penned them as a religious poem. There is probably no truth in the legend that Newton put them to a melody he had heard on the lips of

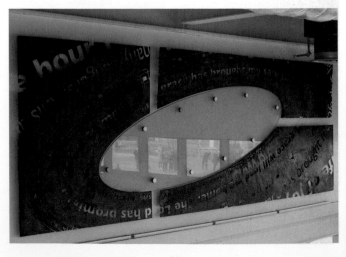

African slaves. It is more likely that the hymn was sung to various tunes until William Walker hit on a traditional tune (New Britain) as the ideal accompaniment in 1835.

Newton had sailed on slave ships from an early age and was engaged as a slave agent in Sierra Leone, where he worked hard to 'tight pack' every vessel despite the inevitable death toll. Greedy, licentious and foul-mouthed, he did not appear destined for the ministry. Howling his prayers to God during a storm in 1748, however, he experienced a 'born again' moment ... despite which, he continued to profit from slavery until turning abolitionist in the 1780s. As he subsequently admitted, 'I was once an active instrument in a business at which my heart now shudders.'

Newton's collaboration with the poet William Cowper on *Olney Hymns* resulted in 'Glorious Things of Thee are Spoken', 'How Sweet the Name of Jesus Sounds' and 'Amazing Grace'. Much loved by his congregation and a good friend to Cowper during a life paralysed by insanity ('scrambling in the dark, among rocks and precipices, without a guide'), Newton was, nevertheless, blamed by Robert Southey for contributing to his friend's mental breakdown.

MANTRA OF THE BRONZE BEATLES

'Om Bhur Bhuvah Swah'

Georges Parade, Pier Head, L3 1BY
James Street station or Liverpool One bus station

The bronze statue of The Beatles at the Pier Head is hard to miss but as tourists jostle for position beside their favourite Beatle, their two-dimensional selfies miss the chance to discover a little more about 'the four lads who shook the world'. Clearly a tribute to the Fab Four, this statue conceals four symbolic messages that rarely get the appreciation they deserve.

Inspired by an early photo of the 'lovable moptops' that once dominated the window of HMV's Liverpool ONE store, sculptor Chris Butler commissioned Andy Edwards to produce a version in bronze. With help from family, friends and fans of the band, Andy worked for six months on the material provided and had a silent version of *A Hard Day's Night* running on a loop in his studio to create this pre-megastardom period piece.

Slightly out of step with one another and replicating the on-stage order they took before giving up on live performances, each Beatle carries a totemic feature that sets him apart from the others.

In his cupped hand, John holds two acorns (cast from nuts found in Central Park, a gunshot away from the Dakota Building), which refer to John and Yoko's 'Acorns for Peace' campaign in the late 1960s.

The camera case slung over Paul's shoulder is a reminder of his marriage to photographer Linda Eastman.

Under Ringo's boot, the 'L8' inscription is a link to his birthplace in Toxteth.

Following the band's brief fling with Hare Krishna while on the film set of *Help!*, George went on to become a serious devotee and close inspection of the belt hanging from the statue's back reveals some Sanskrit verse. When asked about the meaning of the text, Andy says that it was inspired by an afternoon visit to his studio while he was working on George's coat. Three gong performers from Liverpool turned up with various gongs, including a 6ft-diameter relic from George's old school, and began to play. Potters from across the Wedgwood factory found themselves drawn to the hypnotic reverberations and, as the performance ended with a rendition of the *Gayatri Mantra*, 'many were too emotional to speak, inexplicably moved ... somewhere else', says Andy. It took another full day's work to inscribe the prayer onto George's belt.

It was common for Renaissance sculptors to carve their names on sashes. Respectful of the team effort involved in his projects, however, Andy rejects the practice of adding his own signature.

MEMORIAL TO HEROES OF THE MARINE ENGINE ROOM

One of England's first monuments to honour the sacrifice of working men

St Nicholas Place, Pier Head, L3 1QW
James Street station or Liverpool One bus station

The Pier Head is littered with memorials: famous pop stars, war heroes and the odd astronomer vie for our attention, but the monument in honour of those who gave their lives below decks is almost unique because it pays tribute to an anonymous and much ignored group of war heroes. Originally commissioned in 1912 by the White Star Line (see page 48), it was intended to commemorate the 35 engineers who stuck to their posts to maintain the 29 furnaces powering the lights, wireless telegraph and lifeboats as the *Titanic* sank beneath the ice flows of the North Atlantic. However, later disasters at sea (the *Empress of Ireland* and the *Lusitania*), plus the huge casualty rate during the First World War, called for strokes from a broader brush.

Designed by Sir William Goscombe John, it is regarded as one of the first monuments in England to honour the sacrifice of working men. Beneath the 14.5m obelisk are life-sized figures representing our heroes: stokers on the east face and engineers on the west. Above their heads at each corner are depictions of the classical elements caught up in the tragedy: Earth (NE), Water (NW), Fire (SE) and Air (SW). Gilded sunrays, four sea maidens grasping breech buoys and a golden torch flame at the summit complete the decoration.

According to *Historic England*, 'The memorial had a considerable influence upon the design of post-1919 war memorials, particularly in respect of the portrayal of the ordinary man or woman, rather than of members of social or military elites'. It is considered one of the most artistically-significant memorials to the *Titanic* disaster on either side of the Atlantic. In 1912, the *Daily Sketch* commented that 'the ... Liverpool memorial to the *Titanic* Engineers should be a national one, and there is in contemplation a river-side scheme that would surpass, in architectural beauty, the Statue of Liberty in New York'.

Hidden from the public for almost 60 years, and still unknown to most people, is a plaque in the main entrance of the Philharmonic Hall dedicated to the memory of the band who 'bravely continued playing to soothe the anguish of their fellow passengers until the ship sank in the deep'. The 'Phil' was destroyed by fire in 1933 but the plaque was one of the few relics to survive. After the 1995 refurb, it was rescued from a backstage corridor and restored to public view.

PRINCES DOCK DRINKING FOUNTAIN

The father of drinking fountains

William Jessop Way, L3 1QZ
www.liverpoolmonuments.co.uk/drinking/melly.html
James Street station or 10 minutes from Liverpool One bus station

At the southern end of Princes Dock, the small fountain adorned with a lion's head within the dock wall is Liverpool's earliest drinking fountain. It was erected by Charles Pierre Melly (1829–1888) in 1854 as part of a citywide project to provide the populace with fresh drinking water.

A committed Unitarian, Melly founded the North End Domestic Mission, supported Ragged Schools for the poor and funded the first night school for working men in Beaufort Street. He assisted Hulley in the building of the Myrtle Street Gymnasium and founding of the Olympic Games in Liverpool (see page 198) – anyone needing a breather during the marathon could take a break on one of the many public benches he erected across town.

As chairman of the Parks & Gardens Committee, Melly was also instrumental in the creation of Sefton Park but is best known for the introduction of fresh water through a network of polished red granite drinking fountains. Aware of the dangers of contaminated water and the fact that fresh water was only available to householders who could afford it, Melly was appalled at the sight of dockworkers and immigrants drinking from horse troughs or (even worse) going to the alehouse, where beer had long been recognised as a healthy alternative to water.

Of the 43 fountains provided by Melly, only 9 survive (see website opposite). One of them can be found further along the dock road on Bath Street. To get a sense of what these drinking fountains actually looked like, the restoration on Woolton Road (near the Halfway House) is the bee's knees.

'Those whom the Gods wish to destroy they first make mad'

According to the New Testament, 'For whom the Lord loveth he chasteneth' and this odd inscription can be found on Charles Pierre Melly's memorial tablet in the Unitarian Church (see page 202). Perhaps it was no more than a popular biblical proverb, but Melly endured a lifetime battle with depression and in 1888 this unsung local hero brought his torment to an end with a single shot from his own pistol ... It is possible that, when deciding on the text for his memorial, his friends were commenting on the man's more personal struggles.

What goes around, comes around

In 2018, eco campaign group Sustain called for the reintroduction of public water fountains to help rid the UK of plastic bottles.

WESTERN APPROACHES HQ

Britain's best-kept WW2 secret

1–3 Rumford Street, Exchange Flags, L2 8SZ
0151 227 2008
www.liverpoolwarmuseum.co.uk
info@westernapproaches.org.uk
10am–4pm (book online or by phone)
James Street station or Liverpool One bus station

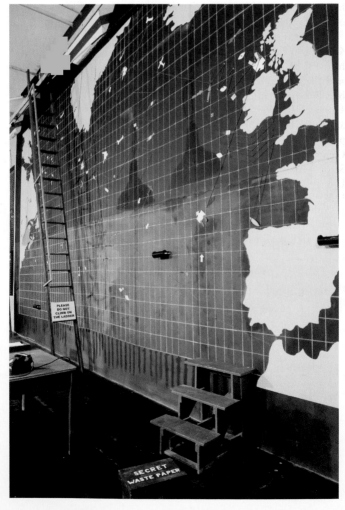

For anyone seeking to escape the incessant intrusions of their mobile phone, the Switchboard Room of the Western Approaches Command is the ideal retreat. Known as the 'Fortress', the windowless, bombproof bunker on Rumford Street was constructed with 3-ft walls beneath a roof that is 7 ft thick and covers 55,000 ft^2 (5,110 m^2). Barely altered since its closure (and not to everyone's taste), the bunker/museum offers an unpolished, authentic trip down memory lane. As you pass through the rabbit warren of corridors, communication chambers and sleeping quarters, it is easy to imagine that the 400 operators of the radios, teleprinters and telephone exchange on show have just popped out for a cuppa and a Wet Nelly (a moist Liverpool fruit cake).

The construction crew were told it was to be a 'restaurant' and the 400 souls who worked here for the duration of the war were forbidden by the Official Secrets Act from disclosing its true purpose. As Churchill said, 'In war-time, truth is so precious that she should always be attended by a bodyguard of lies.' As an island under siege, Britain depended on 1 million tons of imports every week to sustain the war effort and, as a major port overlooking the Western Approaches, Liverpool was of particular strategic importance. Churchill established his Command Centre here for what was to be the longest continual conflict of the Second World War. He later admitted that the 'wolf packs' of German U-boats were 'the only thing that really frightened me during the war'. It is probably no exaggeration to say that the Battle of the Atlantic and HQ's role within it were crucial in defeating Hitler.

The cracking of the Enigma code allowed HQ to decrypt radio and teleprinter communications and second-guess the attacking formations deployed by Admiral Dönitz. Consequently, Admiral Sir Max Horton organised his escorts into 'support groups' and 'hunter-killer groups' to protect the convoys and prevent the 'wolf packs' from forming in the first place.

Hard to believe, in today's world of satellite reconnaissance and drone technology, the elastic string stretched across pins on a giant Plotting Board represented the nerve centre of Britain's wartime defence system. The hotline phone that connected HQ directly to the War Cabinet was housed in a soundproof booth and protected by an armed guard. It is one of only two in the country still in existence.

The Cruel Sea by Nicholas Monsarrat is a fictionalised account of the author's time aboard the *Campanula* during the Battle of the Atlantic.

ORIEL CHAMBERS

'One of the most remarkable buildings of its date in Europe ... unbelievably ahead of its time'

14 Water Street, L2 8TD
James Street station or Liverpool One bus station

Set back from the river on one of Liverpool's original Seven Streets is Oriel Chambers, an architectural treasure that Nikolaus Pevsner regarded as 'one of the most remarkable buildings of its date in Europe ... unbelievably ahead of its time' on account of its cast-iron frame and boxed-out oriel windows.

Restricted access means that your best option is to admire it from the steps of the India Buildings opposite. Cross the street and discover a gated side entrance (Oriel Close) that was once the entrance to the well-respected Oriel Restaurant. The restaurant closed and the gate is locked but to get a flavour of the place, take a coffee and cake break in the basement cafe at No. 16 (A Small Fish in a Big Pond), which is part of the same building.

When, in 1839, Harvey Lonsdale Elmes won the competition to design St George's Hall, it set in train a series of coincidences that were

to transform the face of modern architecture. One of the unsuccessful competitors was a local builder-cum-architect called Peter Ellis. Clearly hurt by the decision, Ellis published, at his own expense, copies of his Rejected Designs for presentation to the project's subscribers as a reminder of what might have been.

Ellis spent the next 20 years designing less imposing buildings: a school, a dispensary, terraced housing on Great George Square (now demolished) and his own homes at 78 Canning Street and, then, next door at 40 Falkner Square.

Then, in July 1863, a fire destroyed the Covent Buildings and Ellis was commissioned to design something to replace it. His fireproof design for what was now to be called Oriel Chambers produced the world's first metal-framed glass curtain-walled building, incorporating over 50 oriel windows to maximise natural light.

Unfortunately, the architectural establishment were not ready for the 'functionalism over grandeur' perspective introduced by the use of new materials. Articles lampooning 'the oddest building in Liverpool ... a cellular habitation for the human insect', or 'a kind of greenhouse architecture gone mad', called into question Ellis' professional competence and left his reputation in tatters. An infamous (and anonymous) sideswipe in the *Porcupine* newspaper decried 'the large agglomeration of protruding plate-glass bubbles' as 'a vast abortion ... a sight to make the angels weep ... shapeless, spiritless pinnacles, all is bad'.

Undeterred, Ellis began work on 16 Cook Street, which grabbed the attention of a young American student thrown there by chance. He returned to the US and introduced Ellis' ideas to the founding members of the Chicago School, keen to get to work on rebuilding the city after the Great Fire of 1871. Without doubt, the general use of steel frames and oriel windows in Chicago's first skyscrapers reflects Ellis' designs.

The world's first paternoster lift

Oriel Chambers is home to the world's first paternoster lift (so named because the mechanism resembles a string of rosary beads), to a design by Ellis. The lift is a chain of open compartments in constant motion, allowing passengers to hop on and off at any floor.

The initials 'TA' on the gable end of Oriel Chambers are those of the original owner, Rev. Thomas Anderson. 'Stand Sure', the family motto, can also be seen.

Detective work by Graham Jones has revealed that 25 & 27 Catharine Street were also designed by Ellis. It is also speculated that he collaborated on 59 Bold Street and 1 Upper Duke Street.

EDITIONS ART GALLERY

The world's smallest skyscraper

16 Cook Street, L2 9RF
www.editionsltd.net/index.html
Mon–Fri 10am–5.30pm, Sat 11am–4pm
Tours operate during Heritage Open Days
James Street station or Liverpool One bus station

As home to the Editions Art Gallery, 16 Cook Street is open to the public and well worth a visit, if only to gain access to an original Peter Ellis building. With the criticism of his peers still ringing in his ears after Oriel Chambers (see page 34), Ellis set about his second modernist creation. Sharples describes it as having a 'tall, narrow front divided into three great arches ... The proportions are those of a warehouse ... there is an amazing amount of plate glass to stonework so that the façade resembles one huge mullioned window.'

As with Oriel Chambers, the idea was to give the office staff the benefit of natural light and reduce the cost of artificial lighting (neighbouring buildings had a 'window opening to wall surface area' of 20%, Cook Street has over 50%). No lift this time, but a glazed cast-iron spiral staircase which dominates the entrance.

During its construction, one visitor had been a very young John Wellborn Root, sent to his father's office in Liverpool to escape the Civil War. On his return to America, he studied architecture and joined Louis Sullivan (another possible admirer of Ellis) in founding the Chicago School. Root's Rookery Building (now the oldest standing high-rise in Chicago) was inspired by Cook Street and, according to Gillian Ward, features an 'oriel stair tower ... of which 16 Cook St must be the precursor'. Given the influence of Ellis' metal frames and interior daylighting (not to mention the invention of the paternoster lift) on American architecture, Quentin Hughes has speculated that Ellis could have become famous had he moved across the pond.

Nevertheless, the common belief that Ellis was broken by his critics and deserted architecture for a dull life as 'an obscure civil engineer' does not stand up to scrutiny. He designed at least two public buildings in the 1870s and patented several important inventions, including his 'mechanical elevator', a flushing toilet, breech-loading and needle-exploding firearms, secure letter boxes and a turnstile system on the omnibus to deter fraud among the bus crew.

Thanks to the efforts of post-war critics, Ellis' reputation has now been restored. Simon Harratt hails him as 'the most remarkable Liverpool architect of the mid-19th century'. In a final riposte to Charles Reilly (founder of the Liverpool School of Architecture and one of Ellis' major critics), the *International Dictionary of Architects and Architecture* (1993) awarded Ellis global recognition but omitted Reilly altogether.

The most detailed biography is *In the Footsteps of Peter Ellis* by Robert Ainsworth and Graham Jones. Or try Anthony Quinn's *The Rescue Man*, which features the imagined diary of a 19th-century Liverpool architect.

YE HOLE IN YE WALL

Liverpool's oldest pub?

4 Hackins Hey, L2 2AW
0151 227 3809
yeholeinyewall.weebly.com
Mon–Sat 12 noon–11pm, Sun 12 noon–10.30pm
Moorfields station or any bus into town, then head for Dale Street

Built on an old Quaker burial ground in 1726, Ye Hole in Ye Wall claims to be Liverpool's oldest pub and features a first-floor cellar (to avoid disturbing the neighbours below) and a ladies' toilet behind the bar.

As a coaching house, it would have been very much part of Liverpool's rise as a port and retains interesting features from the past 300 years, including the ghost of a Spanish sailor murdered by a press gang for refusing the King's shilling and evidence of a Men Only policy that survived until 1977 (hence the Ladies inconveniently squeezed behind the bar). As buildings, the Childwall Abbey Hotel and the Coffee House in Woolton may have older foundations but this is the city's oldest pub.

Other ancient pubs in Merseyside

One of the casualties of Liverpool's Victorian obsession with destroying its medieval heritage is that we do not possess the legacy of ancient public houses we deserve. England has alehouses dating back to the Crusades and it's almost impossible to drive 8 km in Ireland without passing a thatched shack claiming to be 'Ireland's oldest pub'. A quick pub crawl around Merseyside tends to confirm Liverpool's lack of ancient hostelries but a genuine treasure trove awaits on the city's doorstep:

- 16 km to the north, the **Scotch Piper Inn** in Lydiate (Southport Road, L31 4HD) is a Grade II Listed thatched beauty. It dates from 1320, which makes it the oldest pub in Lancashire. Originally named the Royal Oak on account of the tree around which the pub was built, it is said to have taken its current name during the Jacobite rebellion in 1745, when an injured Highland piper was given asylum and ended up marrying the landlord's daughter. Remnants of the old oak are still part of the infrastructure and the internal features retain their character despite a fire in 2016 which destroyed the thatched roof. The pub was reopened in 2017 following a £140,000 refurbishment.

- On the Wirral, the **Wheatsheaf Inn** in Raby (Raby Mere Road, Wirral, CH63 4JH) is recorded as being built in 1611 although it may be a rebuild of an older pub which burned down. Legend has it that a young woman died in the fire and continues to haunt the place. She must have been on her day off when we paid a visit.

- Further to the south, Chester has an embarrassment of riches in the Olde Worlde department with one or two making a mess of the transition. The oldest, by common consent, is the **Pied Bull** (57 Northgate Street, CH1 2HQ), which can be traced back to 1155. It became a coaching house and still retains its 500-year-old staircase. Not to be outdone, this inn boasts at least two ghosts, one of whom has made it onto YouTube accompanied by a spooky soundtrack. What happens when they bump into each other has yet to be recorded but the advice, should you wish to book a room, is to steer clear of No. 9.

- To the east of Liverpool, even Warrington can boast a genuine antique. The **Barley Mow** (29 Old Market Place, WA1 1QB) dates from 1561 and despite a few alterations retains an imposing half-timbered frontage as well as some period paintings and furniture.

TEAGLE CRANE AT HACKINS HEY

The days of drag and drop

Hackins Hey (opp. Ye Hole In Ye Wall), L2 2AW
James Street or Moorfields stations or Liverpool One bus station

Anyone wishing to see the largest hydraulic crane of its type in the world, with a 10-tonne bucket and a £1.8m price tag, would need permission from the Port of Garston to witness the Mantsinen 200M

in action but, off Dale Street, a much smaller version of the species survives. This one is called a teagle crane and dates from the Victorian era, when office buildings often doubled as warehouses.

Designed by Frost & Strutt, this belt-driven relic would have served the basement storehouse via a trapdoor that is still clearly visible. This may have been part of the business conducted at Queen Buildings above or a separate tenancy for a local trader. The pineapple motif on the crane's top could be an allusion to Liverpool's exotic trading links. Either way, it is a very handsome reminder of a time when produce from the docks was transported by carters (see the Waiting statue of a working horse near the Museum of Liverpool) and stored in local warehouses for rapid dispatch.

The greatest painter–scientist in the history of art?

A century earlier, on Dale Street, in a house no longer standing at an address never recorded, Britain's greatest painter of horses was born. A week later, he was baptised in the Church of Our Lady and Saint Nicholas. In 1735, George Stubbs' dad moved the family's currier business to the junction of Ormond Street and Lombard Street, probably on the spot where Lombard Chambers now stands (more teagles).

Little is known of George's early life but we are told that his drawing skills were encouraged by a local surgeon (Dr Holt). Following a brief flirtation with the family trade, George negotiated himself an apprenticeship with painter Hamlet Winstanley, copying pictures at Knowsley Hall. The relationship broke down and the young artist moved to York, where he painted portraits and studied anatomy. During a return visit to Liverpool, he produced his only painting on home soil to have survived: a portrait of James Stanley that hangs in the Walker Art Gallery.

Back in York, Stubbs provided the illustrations for Dr Burton's *Essay Towards a Complete New System of Midwifery* (1751), which almost ended his career. The drawings were based on the dissection of a woman who had died in childbirth and Stubbs was held in 'vile reknown' across the city. Unperturbed, he set about bleeding horses to death, dissecting them and assembling the set of engravings that would make his name, *Anatomy of the Horse*. Copies of both can be found in the archives at Liverpool Central Library.

A stone's throw from George Stubbs' birthplace, the Walker Art Gallery displays some of the artist's most famous works, including *Molly Longlegs*, *Horse Frightened by a Lion* and *The Lincolnshire Ox*.

NELSON'S SWORD

Or is it?

Liverpool Town Hall, High St, L2 3SW
0151 233 3020
www.liverpoolcityhalls.co.uk/town-hall/your-visit/
The Town Hall runs monthly tours and annual Open Days
Also see events page on website or call to arrange a visit
5 minutes from James Street station and Liverpool One bus station

Amongst the few who know of its existence, the ceremonial blade which sits in a display cabinet in the Town Hall to the right of the main staircase is known as Nelson's Sword. This is easy to appreciate in a city whose merchants valued highly the prospect of passage on the high seas free from French and Spanish privateers and is compounded by an official explanation which claims that the sword 'was to be presented by the merchants and Corporation of Liverpool to honour and commemorate Admiral Nelson as the "Victor of the Battle of the Nile"' but, due to his death at Trafalgar, Nelson's second in command (Collingwood) was invited to receive it on behalf of his friend.

The sword must have been truly cursed as, following his acceptance of the honour, Collingwood himself died before he could attend the presentation 'which is why the sword remains in Liverpool Town Hall today'.

However, on closer inspection, this interpretation is contradicted by the inscription on the sword itself which suggests that there were two funds:

one to erect a monument to 'the immortal memory of ... Nelson (which dominates Exchange Flags) and a separate one to honour, with a sword, 'his gallant successor ... Lord Collingwood, for his heroic conduct in the never to be forgotten naval engagement at Trafalgar'.

This has been confirmed by Commander Mark Barton who says that 'the sword was completed in 1807 and presumably presented to (Collingwood's) widow around 1810'. It remained in the family until being sold at auction in 1899 and again during WW1 to raise funds for the Red Cross. At the end of the war it was purchased and presented to Major John Utting (Lord Mayor of Liverpool) 'in gratitude for his work ... in raising £13m during War Bond Week'. Admiralty librarian Jenny Wraight concurs with this view and adds that 'it was usual if a naval officer died for any prize money, honours or awards that may have been due to him to go to his nearest kin' as was the case with the Lloyd's Patriotic Fund silver vases which were presented to all the admirals involved in Trafalgar. This would explain why the sword ended up in the possession of the Collingwood family and debunks the notion that the sword has been sitting in the town hall for two hundred years awaiting collection.

The Northumbrian who saved the nation

'Old Cuddy' was honoured for seeing out the victory at Trafalgar but is largely forgotten today. His tomb stands in St Paul's Cathedral alongside that of his friend.

THE SANCTUARY STONE

'A unique relic of Liverpool's medieval origins'

Castle Street, opposite Number 22 L2 0UP
5 minutes from James Street station and Liverpool One bus station

Opposite number 22 on Castle street, generations of scousers scurrying to work have hardly noticed the existence on the pavement of an insignificant lump of black stone resembling a giant blob of chewing gum.

According to senior archaeologist Mark Adams of National Museums Liverpool: "The Sanctuary Stone is a unique relic of Liverpool's medieval origins, being the only extant element of the medieval landscape to have survived to the present within the city's historic core" and can be found beneath a wall-mounted plaque. It is the only surviving boundary marker for the Town Fair which was held twice a year dating back to the 13th C.

During the fair, it was possible for thieves and debtors to avoid arrest so long as they did not stray beyond its boundary. A pound coin was interred when the stone was relaid in 2011 to match the pre-decimal pennies put in place on the two previous excavations in 1937 and 1947.

Named after the moated castle which dominated what is now Derby Square for almost 500 years, Castle Street is one of the original Seven Streets of Liverpool but unfortunately contains no trace of its medieval claim to fame. Like so much of this Victorian city, its past has been obliterated by forceful development keen to proclaim its ascendency and embarrassed by reminders of its humble origins. Built around 1235, the castle was a commanding structure designed by someone with a siege mentality to contain a courtyard, orchard, dovecot, brewery and bake house. The site of various conflicts, it was captured by Prince Rupert during the Civil War only to be retaken by Cromwell a couple of months later. Eventually demolished in the 1700s, it was replaced by St George's Church which, in its turn, made way for the po-faced Victoria Monument.

Excavations in the 1920s revealed the old moats, one of which is still to be found beneath Castle Moat House on Derby Square. Apart from the eponymous street name and a commemorative plaque on Victoria's rear end, there is nothing here to indicate that Liverpool ever had its own garrison although anyone wishing to catch a glimpse of castle life at the tatty end of its existence could visit a scaled model of the ruins at Rivington commissioned by Lord Leverhulme in 1912.

Edward Litherland demolished the Castle and monopolised the use of the reclaimed stone. Remnants can be seen inside the Bluecoat (see page 14) where the old building abuts the new. The dates suggest he began helping himself to the stone before he was legally entitled to.

MACE ON THE QUEEN VICTORIA STATUE

Member of the British Empire

Derby Square, L2 7ZH
James Street station and Liverpool One bus station

The Victoria Monument on Derby Square has a true-to-life bronze of Queen Victoria by C. J. Allen. Allegorical figures around the base represent Justice, Wisdom, Charity and Peace with a winged figure on the top symbolising Fame (the queen's, presumably) while the groups around the podium represent Agriculture, Industry, Education and Commerce. In gratitude for the fortunes of Empire bestowed upon a port deriving its wealth from all four, it is not surprising to find Liverpolitans honouring their queen and themselves in this way.

Sharples is in no doubt that 'This was Allen's magnum opus and is one of the most ambitious monuments to the Queen.' It narrowly survived the Blitz and stood as a symbol, among the desolation, of Liverpool's dogged refusal to submit.

To the jaundiced eye of political commentator and activist Owen Jones, it was an offensive celebration of colonialism but others have noted a more mundane cause for offence: viewed from a particular vantage point (opposite, at the junction of Castle Street, is best) the mace looks more like a flaccid penis.

Hopefully the queen's daughter, the Princess Louisa, missed this architectural conceit when she unveiled the statue in 1906, so avoiding the shock of seeing her mum represented as a hermaphrodite.

Recently, Doris McLaren from the Wirral has claimed that her grandad and his two brothers (well-formed wrestlers in the flesh) were used as models by the sculptor – not a proud boast under the circumstances. Also some twit from the safety of the Twittersphere has claimed it was a vengeful prank on behalf of unpaid craftsmen – a good story, but one that makes no sense and, unsurprisingly, has no shred of evidence to support it.

Whatever the truth, Victoria would not have been amused by this little optical illusion as she exhibited great distaste for masonry representations of the male member in public places ... to the extent that a copy of Michelangelo's David had to be disguised with a detachable plaster-cast fig leaf to save the royal blushes on the queen's visit to the V&A in 1857.

Villa Victoria

During the Liverpool Biennial 2002, the statue made a comeback as an art installation, when Japanese conceptual artist Tatsurou Bashi transformed the monument by constructing a fully furnished hotel room and reception area around it. Visitors found themselves on the same level as the queen and those who felt the urge to splurge could pay to spend the night with Her Majesty – it was booked out.

ORIGINAL FEATURES
AT 30 JAMES STREET

'The streaky-bacon building'

Albion House, L2 7PQ
0151 236 0166
rmstitanichotel.co.uk
James Street station and Liverpool One bus station

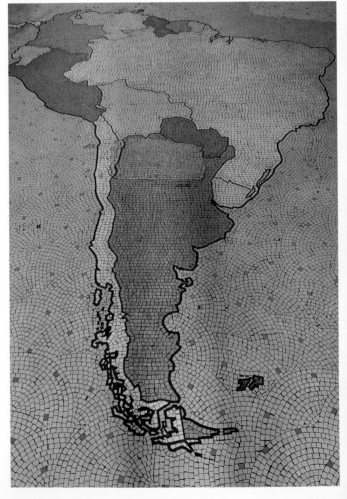

Built in red brick and Portland stone in the late 1880s by Richard Norman Shaw (and repeating features in his New Scotland Yard), 30 James Street boutique hotel was once the head office of the White Star Line. Unlike the Titanic Hotel, it has a genuine connection to the tragedy: take the stairs to appreciate the photographic recollections of *Titanic* times gone by, including sad portraits of those who went down with the ship.

The *Titanic* was conceived and registered in the ground-floor offices (now the Grand Hall) and news of its fate was transmitted to desperate family members from the second-floor balcony (now Room 22). The bent security bars on the cast-iron entrance gates are said to bear witness to the crush created by angry relatives desperate for news of their loved ones (one in ten of the crew were local).

The Albion building also provides the backdrop to Bill Tidy's funniest spot gag ('Is there any news of the iceberg?'), which would have seen him lynched back in 1912 for sheer bad taste.

After a spell as offices for the Blue Star Line, the building ended up in mothballs until 2013, when Signature Living gave it an expensive 'make-over'. The restoration has revealed several original features (cast-iron girders and stanchions, ceilings of Ruabon terracotta, wall safes by Milner and a wonderful tiled floor in the entrance portraying destinations in South America). The aim was to transform a Victorian office block into a boutique hotel, spa and restaurant, however, and the limitations of working within a listed building are clear to see.

Apart from the Grand Hall and the Presidential Suite (which takes up an entire wing and enjoys its own balcony), most office spaces were poorly served by tiny windows that simply added to the gloom (see pages 74 and 90). Taking advantage of this, J. P. Morgan's basement vault has been converted into a dorm for hen parties, where the last thing residents are interested in is a room with a view. On the floors above, an attempt has been made to recreate a below-decks experience while the rooftop restaurant and cocktail bar offer great views over the Albert Dock, the Three Graces and Derby Square.

Alfred Gwynne Vanderbilt, heir to the family empire, cancelled his passage on the *Titanic* at the last minute and was originally listed as 'lost'. His luck finally ran out three years later, when he went down with the *Lusitania* instead.

DREAM PASSAGE

'We are such stuff as dreams are made on'

Platform 2 of James Street station
James Street, L2 7PQ

James Street station has its main entrance on James Street (surprise, surprise!) but on Water Street, close by the India Buildings (erstwhile home to the splendid Holt's Arcade), is a side entrance that is unknown to all but the most regular commuters. Open during weekday rush hours, it spends most of its time closed to the public. The passageway retains many original features: stone paving worn down by years of use, traditional tiling and copies of retro poster adverts interspersed with maps of the '7 Streets' area on brass plaques that act as a timeline of the waterfront over the past 500 years.

But the real surprise is to be found on the Wirral-bound track, where the closed platform 2 is reserved for emergency use only. Nevertheless, anyone on platform 3 with a shred of curiosity can peer through the gloom to make out a bas-relief sculpture bursting through the Victorian tiling on the opposite platform.

As the plaque identifying the artists is situated at the foot of the stairs

to platform 2, it is hardly surprising that even those who have wondered at its purpose as they await the 17.52 to New Brighton have no idea who created it or why they bothered.

As it turns out, the piece was commissioned by Merseyrail to celebrate its 100th anniversary and the return of the Tall Ships in 1992. The artists, Tim Chalk and Paul Grimes, were given a completely open brief: the only restriction on subject matter was that it should have nothing to do with trains or The Beatles. Fractured references to the world above jostle alongside hints of mythical creatures and lost civilisations.

According to Tim: 'The work is deliberately enigmatic and open to personal interpretations. Passengers on the opposite platform are often in their own private bubble and the artwork is there to provide a launch pad for their imagination. Situated in a physical passage, it represents a rite of passage from Birth to Death. The first panel (a mother and baby) shows life springing from the earth and the last shows it returning to the earth (a figure dissolving into the sculpture), while the two middle panels show the life of the imagination and subconscious and the life of rational thought. All the panels incorporate details from local architecture above ground. The whole work is intended to create the sense of archaeological discovery, "the excavation of the subconscious of the city".'

Freud would have had a field day!

CLAY RELIEF OF A GORILLA

'Art is to architecture as lipstick is to a gorilla'

Cavern Walks, Harrington Street, L2 6RE
James Street station or Liverpool One bus station

The front entrance to Cavern Walks is on Mathew Street where terracotta reliefs of doves and roses, designed by Cynthia Lennon, adorn the façade. But slip out the back into Harrington Street and look up to find a surprising keystone of a gorilla with a compact mirror engrossed in the act of applying her lippy. When designing the building in 1984, architect Dave Backhouse added this ceramic sideswipe at Norman Foster, who had famously complained that public art in contemporary architecture was like putting 'lipstick on the face of a gorilla'.

The basement of the Cavern Club is a replica

The Cavern Club is forever associated with the rise of The Beatles. What many visitors fail to realise is that the basement is a replica: the famous original was demolished to make way for a ventilation shaft that British Rail never built. The renovation was turned sideways, expanded and given a new entrance ... the fire exit on Mathew Street is all that remains of the original.

NEARBY

The bust of Carl Jung   (22)

Long before Mathew Street became world-famous as home to the Cavern Club, the psychoanalyst and guru Carl Jung had a dream that featured Liverpool (a city he'd never seen) as a dark and miserable place 'obscured by rain, fog, smoke and dimly lit darkness'. It was, however, blessed with a pool of water: here, on an island, a solitary tree blossomed, standing in the sunlight and representing 'the source of light'. Popping onto his own couch for some quick self-analysis, Jung discovered among all the misery and despair (his current state of mind) 'a vision of unearthly beauty', indicating life's purpose. Liverpool, wrote Jung, is 'the pool of life'. To mark his Scouse epiphany, a bust was placed on the wall of No. 18 in 1987 (replaced in 1993 with the present version). Convinced it was part of the interstellar ley line (connecting Iceland to New Guinea), artist and musician Bill Drummond spent a 17-hour vigil on a nearby manhole cover to channel its force.

Liverpool's No. 1 Hall of Fame

There is more to life than music and more to Liverpool than The Beatles. At the top of Mathew Street is a tribute to local artists who made it to No. 1 ... the earliest hit being 'How Much is That Doggie in the Window?', a tacky little ditty so awful that '50s singer Lita Roza (who recorded it) refused to perform it live.

HOLY CROSS MEMORIAL GARDEN ㉓

'Small in extent, yet great and glorious in tradition'

Standish Street, L3 2BL (north of the city centre, at the end of Tithebarn Street)
Merseyrail: 2-min stroll from Moorfields station
10-min walk from Liverpool One bus station

Now a cul-de-sac of neat bungalows, Standish Street is home to a tiny garden and a plaque marking an ancient stone, a powerfully carved Calvary and Pietà from a demolished church, a sandstone cross from the altar, a foundation stone and some stained glass. Below ground are a couple of time capsules containing additional artefacts from the original church. The carved wooden reredos, Stations of the Cross, oak panelling and doors were transferred to Liverpool Metropolitan Cathedral, while other items have ended up in Oblate parishes locally and across the country.

In medieval times, this was a crossroads for the important trade with Lancashire and Ormskirk. It was marked by an ancient stone that indicated the spot where St Patrick preached to the faithful before departing to rid Ireland of snakes and pagan thought in the 5th century. It was still recorded on a map dated around 1650 but disappeared some time during the 19th century.

In 1860, a church was built on the spot for the Oblate mission. Designed by Pugin, the Church of the Holy Cross became popular with the local Irish and Italian communities and even more so with John Surratt, who holed up there while fleeing the US government on charges of conspiracy to assassinate Lincoln (see following double-page spread).

Almost destroyed during an air raid which claimed the lives of 125 civilians sheltering in the adjoining school, Holy Cross was rebuilt after the Second World War only to fall victim to slum clearance and redevelopment of the Scotland Road area: a congregation of thousands in the 1870s had dwindled to a handful by the end of the millennium and Holy Cross eventually received the Order of the Sacred Wrecking Ball in 2001 as part of an official cull of underused churches. Demolished in 2004, it was replaced by a pretty uninspiring box of apartments which provide an appropriate backdrop to the flyover but an incongruous one for the memorial garden, which is now maintained by the local community.

As local writer Ken Pye points out, the modern close is now home to a site commemorating 'Little Italy', the Church of the Holy Cross and the leaving of Liverpool by St Patrick.

John Surratt: a man who holed up at the Holy Cross Church while fleeing the US government on charges of conspiracy to assassinate Lincoln

Jesuit postmaster, Confederate spy and 'most wanted man in America', John Surratt went on the run following the assassination of Abraham Lincoln in 1865. Surratt was suspected of being a member of the conspiracy led by John Wilkes Booth which included Surratt's own mother whose boarding house was used in the plot. Surratt had been involved in an earlier plan to kidnap Lincoln but was out of town on a spying mission when the assassination took place. With Wilkes Booth tracked down and shot, and four conspirators (including Mary Surratt) executed, Surratt became a wanted man with a $25,000 price on his head. He escaped to Montreal, where he was given refuge by the expat Confederate community and two sympathetic priests until it was safe to take the RMS Peruvian to Liverpool.

Disguised and under an assumed name, Surratt arrived in Liverpool

at the end of September 1865 and, in a pro-Confederacy city where 'every brick is cemented ... with the blood and sweat of negroes' and blessed with a thriving Catholic community, had no problem finding a safe haven. Once again, the Church obliged although his hiding place was an open secret. Despite repeated appeals by the US Vice-Consul ('Such a wretch ought not to escape'), the American government showed little urgency in seeking his extradition and he sailed unhindered to Rome, where he had been recruited into the Papal Zouaves.

According to Sharon Clough of Historic England, there is nothing odd about the role of Holy Cross in harbouring Surratt as 'The Oratory of the Holy Cross was the Roman Catholic clearing house through which ecclesiastical agents passed between the US and the Vatican.' Nevertheless, conspiracy theorists have had a field day suggesting that the Jesuits were behind the assassination of a president who was detested as a heretic (Lincoln had been accused of apostasy) and the leader of the most powerful republic in the world at a time when Rome was under threat from Garibaldi's Risorgimento.

Surratt eventually stood trial in 1867, following his arrest in Egypt, but the charges did not stick and the jury failed to agree a verdict. After a lecture tour which received mixed reviews, he settled down in Baltimore in the US as a teacher and family man. He died at the ripe old age of 72, with Liverpool holding a special place in his heart.

'Other than that, Mrs Lincoln, how did you enjoy the play?'

The Liverpool connection runs a bit deeper than offering an escape route for a wanted man. First, Lincoln's assassin, John Wilkes Booth, was the son of Junius Brutus Booth, who had been a great favourite at Liverpool's Theatre Royal in Williamson Square before deserting his wife and emigrating to the US with Mary Ann Holmes.

Second, there is an oft-repeated legend that Liverpool-born actor Tony Booth is a descendant of Junius' brother, Algernon. This would make for a great story, with Cherie Booth related to an assassin of a US president and married to a UK prime minister; unfortunately, the genealogical evidence doesn't stack up.

Finally, the play Lincoln had gone to see on the night of his assassination (*Our American Cousin*) was made popular by Edward Askew Sothern (from the Priory in Aigburth), with his portrayal of Lord ('Nice but Dim') Dundreary ... although he was not on stage for the fatal performance.

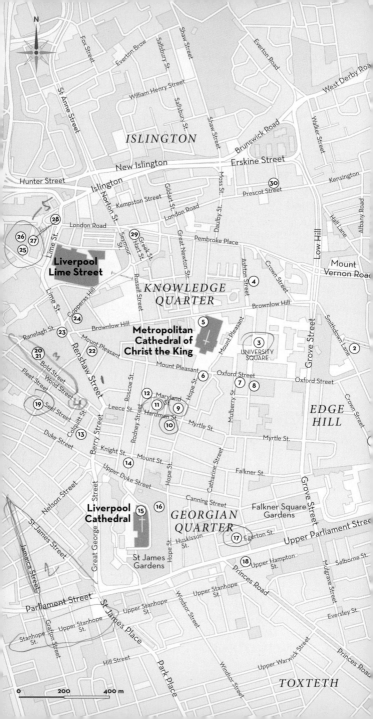

The Georgian Quarter

[Handwritten annotations:]

Next to 3: + Victoria Gallery & Museum
Next to 9: pub
Next to 10: early dc

1. 69A - shop
2. Baltic Triangle - Penvries gallery
3. Bold Street
4. FACT gallery - 88 Wood St + World Museum
5. St Georges Hall + Walker Gallery

CROWN STREET VENTILATION SHAFT

A vestige of the world's first passenger railway station

Crown Street, L7 3LZ
Short walk from University of Liverpool along Myrtle Street to pedestrian walkway into Crown Street Park

Dominating the western corner of Crown Street Park is a huge red brick tower that marks a momentous occasion in railway history it had nothing to do with. Clues to the hidden significance of this otherwise unremarkable scrap of public space can be found in the names given to the adjoining student residences (Stephenson House, the Railyard, the Sidings) and long-overdue signage at the entrance proclaiming it as 'the western terminus of the world's first passenger railway'.

From this spot on 15 September 1830, the very first rail passengers boarded Robert Stephenson's steam locomotive Northumbrian for a 56-km journey to Manchester that would revolutionise mass transportation.

Crown Street was the closest point to the town centre the City Fathers would allow but, after six years of commuters complaining about antiquated horse-drawn transfers into town, Lime Street station replaced it as the main passenger terminus. Crown Street station was relegated to a goods yard until its closure in the 1970s.

While Manchester has retained and transformed the eastern terminus at Liverpool Road into the splendid Science and Industry Museum, four sandstone gateposts on Crown Street are all that remain of the spot where railway history was made.

The main purpose of the L&M railway had been to connect the Cottonopolis of Manchester to Britain's second-largest port and facilitate the transfer of raw materials and goods between the two. This meant that a hand-hewn (2-km) tunnel had to be excavated from nearby Edge Hill junction down to the docks (the first anywhere in the world). Known as the Wapping Tunnel, it ran directly below the station at Crown Street and relied upon gravity and cable to get wagons up and down.

When steam trains replaced this system 60 years later, five ventilation shafts were built along the route to disperse pollution from the tunnel into the air. Only three survive: Blackburne Place, Grenville Street South and this one on Crown Street.

A dockside portal to the Wapping Tunnel can still be found on a cul-de-sac on King's Dock Road indicating the old rail exit to the docks.

The world's oldest operational railway station

With the closure of Liverpool Road and Edge Hill, Broad Green station is now the oldest operational railway station in the world.

FRIENDS OF WILLIAMSON'S TUNNELS

The moles of Edge Hill

Williamson's house site, Mason Street, L7 3EW
Wed & Sun and Open Heritage Days
Tour bookings must be made online:
www.williamsontunnels.com Free entry but membership fees or donations
appreciated
10-min walk from Lime Street station up Brownlow Hill

With around 100,000 visitors a year, the Williamson Tunnels Heritage Centre on Smithdown Lane is a well-known tourist destination, featuring a static display of two excavated tunnels. However, only a street away, the Friends of Williamson's Tunnels (FOWT), a rival group, is a fascinating work very much in progress. Based at the site of Williamson's house, the group took their inspiration from an *Echo* article in 1925 and records of excavations conducted by the army in 1882 and 1907.

We know that Williamson employed men to excavate into the bedrock and had solid arches of brick and stone constructed over the passageways and chambers to create a warren of 'tunnels'. But we don't know why they were built or even how far they stretch as he left no clues as to motive, no scheme of works or maps to record his progress. The predicament is complicated by the fact that over the years following his death, the tunnels were back-filled with industrial waste and household rubbish and then built over. The FOWT's task is to reverse a century of fly-tipping by painstakingly removing the infill a bucket at a time.

Granted a licence to dig in 1998, the human bucket chain of volunteers have been at it ever since. In 2012 their 'epic journey of discovery' began with Big Dig 1 on the Paddington site: it took four years and filled 159 skips with 1,600 tonnes of rubble. The quality of the craftsmanship revealed is remarkable and the scale of the project breathtaking. When they got down to Level 3, the team discovered a huge new chamber some 10.6 metres deep which hits rock bottom at 18 metres below street level.

Almost as soon as this was complete, FOWT started Big Dig 2 on Mason Street. This revealed a stone staircase of 'skilfully carved bull nose buttressed steps' leading to the wine bins and, via a narrow passageway (the Gash), down to what is now called the Banqueting Hall. It is claimed that Williamson invited the city's upper crust to supper only to serve them bacon and beans – those that stormed out missed the sumptuous feast that had secretly been prepared for them next door.

The extraction process has unearthed a treasure trove of Liverpool's rubbish past. Keep an eye out for a Harden Star glass 'fire grenade' – a highly improbable defence against a house fire. Other star exhibits include what became known as 'murder bottles' – early feeders for babies that incubated and transmitted lethal bacteria and contributed significantly to Victorian infant mortality rates.

SQUARES WITH TWO CIRCLES SCULPTURE

One of Barbara Hepworth's most important works

Crown Place, 200 Brownlow Hill, L3 5UE
10-min walk from Lime Street or Central station
Any bus to the University of Liverpool campus

Said to be inspired by Neolithic standing stones, the *Squares with Two Circles* bronze by Barbara Hepworth does not appear out of place fronting a very modern apartment block in the centre of Liverpool University's campus and 6 km away from its nearest Neolithic ancestors (see page 214). Purchased by the university in 1969, it is regarded as one of Hepworth's most important works, with replicas in Yorkshire and Texas. It was originally placed on a platform especially designed by the sculptress to dominate the east side of Abercromby Square but, 45 years later, it was moved as part of landscaping for a luxury student development. This means that it no longer inhabits a public space and is hidden from those of us who thought they knew where it was … to be enjoyed by a tiny community who probably do not know what it is.

This is a good question regarding any work of abstract art where figures (human or otherwise) become simplified into abstract shapes that present us with a puzzle to be worked on rather than worked out. With *Pierced Form* (1931), Hepworth introduced the use of holes within structures to explore the interaction between form and space, sometimes known as the 'Outside/Inside relationship'. Copied by Henry Moore and others, it became the trademark of modernist art and helped establish Hepworth as a world-renowned sculptor in a profession dominated by men.

In the 1950s, Hepworth began working in metals. At first glance, *Squares with Two Circles* seems to reflect the simple geometric design of the Crown Place apartment block that towers above it. On closer inspection, however, its squares are not perfect perpendicular constructions and its rough and slightly convex surface hints at shapes found in nature rather than architecture. Hepworth explained that she was interested in 'the proportion of the sculpture in relation to the human figure and the apertures are placed in relation to human vision'. So is it a body or is it a face? (It has an eye, a gaping mouth and the hint of a nose.) Or is the exploration of form and shape a reference to the dichotomy between physical appearance and the inner self? Like a good joke, maybe great art only works if the punchline is not explained.

Given that Hepworth is one of Britain's greatest 20th-century artists, with a museum dedicated to her work in St Ives and a gallery bearing her name in Yorkshire, it was a bewildering decision to move this important work to such a remote location.

NEARBY

The university has invested in several works of modern art, which are displayed across the campus. Download the Campus Map and Sculpture Walk from the university's website (vgm.liverpool.ac.uk/exhibitions-and-events/tours/walking-tour/) and track them down.

SAVING *ADAGIO*

Time and motion study

Harold Cohen Library, Ashton Street, L69 3DA
15-min walk up Brownlow Hill from Lime Street or Central station
Any bus to the University of Liverpool (many stop on Brownlow Hill)

Anyone turning up at the Philharmonic Hall in the hope of catching the 'rocking and swirling action' of Marianne Forrest's kinetic sculpture is in for a disappointment. *Adagio*, which for twenty years kept time with stars from around the globe, was removed as part of the 2012 refurbishment and transported to the Harold Cohen Library 1 km away.

A 'moving sculpture in brass, aluminium, GRP, copper and silver leaf', it has a fixed base and two moving parts: the wave, which represents music and the listener (it has the profile of a face); and a spiral, affectionately known as 'the sperm'. At an original cost of £40k, this was destined to be very expensive landfill until Prof. Peter Goodhew heard of the plan at a patrons' dinner and decided to do something about it.

A campaign to save the work attracted funds via the Friends of the University and some Kickstarter donations. Oddly enough, the Heritage Lottery covers 'archaeological sites ... stories, festivals, crafts, music, dance and costumes ... landscapes and gardens, oral history and places and objects linked to our industrial, maritime and transport history' but

it does not cover works of art ... moving, static or otherwise.

No matter: how difficult can it be to transfer a sculpture from one side of Brownlow Hill to the other? The answer is: a) very; and b) twice as expensive as first thought.

With help from university librarian Phil Sykes and Janet Beer (the university's proactive vice chancellor), the Main Reading Room at the Harold Cohen Library was identified as the best site to accommodate a 9-metre-long artwork weighing in at 150 kg. With help from the artist, the original contractors were brought back to Liverpool and moved the sculpture to its new home courtesy of a side window. After two years of campaigning, fundraising and stress, the new *Adagio* was unveiled. 'She fits in better than I had hoped,' said Prof. Goodhew, 'and the contrast with the grey wall works very well.' Asked if it had been worth the effort, he replied, 'We saved an artwork, had fun, enhanced my university (IMHO) and met a fascinating sculptor/clockmaker. What's not to like?'

To view the *Adagio* sculpture, simply ask at the library reception desk to be admitted to the Main Reading Room. Due to the slight disturbance created by the motors, the kinetics are only switched on every Friday between 4pm and 4.30pm and not at all during exam periods. So, shhh. Please.

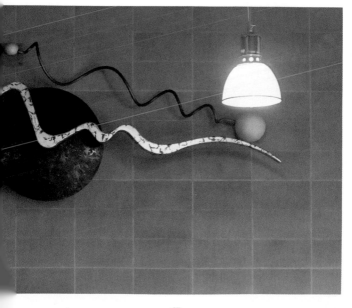

LUTYENS' CRYPT

Liverpool's best kept secret

Liverpool Cathedral
Mount Pleasant, L3 5TQ
www.liverpoolmetrocathedral.org.uk/lutyens-crypt
Mon-Sat 10am-4pm (last visit at 3.30pm)
10-min walk from Lime Street and Central stations
15 min from Liverpool One

Lutyens' model of his giant of a cathedral is on the top floor of the Museum of Liverpool, but if you want some idea of how truly huge it was going to be, take the tour of the crypt. Those who visit to worship or attend the odd beer festival have no idea what treasures are locked away.

With walls of bare brick, granite columns and lined with Travertine marble, it contains two cavernous halls, two chapels plus a Chapel of Relics which guards the earthly remains of three bishops. It is sealed off by a six-ton marble wheel which can be rolled back and forth – clearly a reference to Christ's tomb. On display are detailed drawings and watercolours depicting Lutyens' vision, correspondence between the Archbishop and his architect and photographs recording the development of the site.

At the junction of Brownlow Hill and Mount Pleasant stands the site of what was once the largest workhouse in Britain and the proposed

location for Lutyens' Metropolitan Cathedral. The first was demolished before the war and the latter never built. The intention had been to build 'a cathedral in our time' of such magnitude that it would surpass St Peter's in Rome and transcend the efforts of Giles Gilbert Scott at the other end of Hope Street. But with only the crypt completed, post war reconstruction meant the project was mothballed, as was a scaled-down version by Scott's brother, Adrian. In 1960, Sir Frederick Gibberd's competition-winning design ticked all the boxes; it would be built in 5 years, at a cost of no more than £1m and reflect the commitment of Vatican II 'to open the windows of the church and let in some fresh air'.

On the back of his Harlow New Town triumph, he came up with a very modern design which was built in five years but at a cost of £2.2m.

His achievement (2 out of 3, not bad) still splits architectural opinion down the middle; a real Marmite of a building, it is known to all as Paddy's Wigwam.

There but for the Grace of God ...

While you are admiring the stalled splendour of the 'Greatest Building never built' spare a thought for John Jackson, 'the demon bowler' of Notts and England cricket teams, widely considered to be the best bowler of the 19th century. He died in the workhouse destitute and alone in 1901.

LIVERPOOL MEDICAL INSTITUTION

'So teach us to number our days, that we may apply our hearts unto wisdom'

114 Mount Pleasant, L3 5SR
0151 709 9125
See website for opening times and events: www.lmi.org.uk
Access is generally restricted to members and academics but open on Heritage Open Days and for public lectures. Group tours can be booked by phone or online
10-min walk uphill from Lime Street station or any bus stopping on Hardman Street or Brownlow Hill

The Council Room of the magnificent LMI building is home to a museum of medical artefacts under the watchful eye of an ancient 28-day longcase clock. The 'Old Doctor' entered this world around 1680, a date verified when he appeared on the Antiques Roadshow and his provenance was confirmed. The clock was commissioned by Silvester Richmond, the first qualified doctor to practise in Liverpool, and remained in the family until 1965, when it was donated to the country's first Medical Institute on Mount Pleasant.

A private library for medical practitioners, the Liverpool Medical Institution originated as a 'Surgeons' Book Club' in the 1760s and then as the Medical Library on Shaw's Brow. In 1837, it moved to its present neoclassical, purpose-built home founded by Dr John Rutter on the site

of abolitionist William Roscoe's birthplace, the Bowling Green pub. The library is a repository of medical knowledge dating back to 1536 and contains 12,800 books, 18,000 bound journals and a unique collection of pamphlets that cram the shelves over two floors. The upper floor also houses a beautiful 120-seater lecture theatre used, in its day, for 'living exhibits' (freak shows for medical practitioners at which patients would display rare medical conditions for diagnosis by a panel of doctors).

If you're lucky enough to book a tour, keep an eye out for some real gems: inside the impressive main entrance, the John Rutter Memorial Tablet, rescued from St Peter's Church, adorns the wall, while close by the reception desk sits a secret ballot box used by the members to vote on new applicants. Beautifully carved in mahogany, it has a drawer of coloured bone counters (rather than black balls) that the members would cast inside the chamber to the left (YES) or right (NO). Interestingly, this is dated 1822 ... 50 years before the general electorate were guaranteed the same privilege by the Ballot Act.

Back in the Council Room, the skull of a Mongol warrior (with someone else's chin) grins at you, reminding us of the Victorians' fascination with eugenics, anthropology and what writer Marek Kohn terms 'Race Galleries'. In a nearby cabinet is a beautifully preserved 'warm tobacco smoke enema'. Telling people what they want to hear is known colloquially as 'blowing smoke up your arse' but the practice has some medical foundation as tobacco smoke administered by the back door via a set of bellows was used for 'the recovery of persons apparently drowned'.

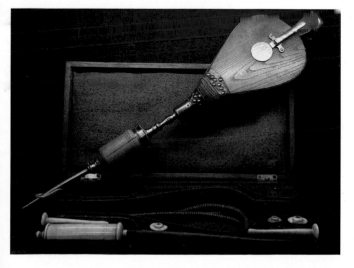

THE *QUICKENING* SCULPTURE

Mitzi's knockers

Cambridge Street, L7 7EE
15-min walk up Brownlow Hill from Central or Lime Street station
Removed for renovation,will return in 2020

Hiding in the courtyard between the Civic Design building and the Cambridge pub is a fabulous Portland stone sculpture by the New York-born sculptress Mitzi Cunliffe. Called *The Quickening*, it features what looks to be a dove nestling in the palm of a cupped hand. Cunliffe had moved to Manchester following her marriage to an academic at the university and used the garage at the family home in Didsbury as a workshop. Two of her works were selected for the 1951 Festival of Britain, on the back of which she was commissioned to produce this work for the newly built and pretty grim Department of Civic Design.

A pair of well-crafted bronze door handles (also by Cunliffe) go some way to offsetting the post-war functionality of what is home to 'the oldest school of planning in the world'. Today's graduates are promised a degree that develops 'the theoretical and practical skills necessary to become an agent for change on the global stage'. Hopefully they don't take too much inspiration from the building itself.

Mitzi Cunliffe: a female garage artist in Didsbury

Cunliffe was prolific. Her best-known creation is the BAFTA Mask – probably one of the most coveted trophies on the planet. Her own favourite, however, was a pierced bronze screen (*The Wars of the Roses*) commissioned for the Red Rose Restaurant in Lewis's Depart-ment Store as part of its post-war restoration. Unfortunately, the store closed in 1985 and the upper floor was sealed off (see page 108). Cunliffe wasted little time buying back the work and transporting it to her holiday home in the Côte d'Azur.

In the 1960s, she turned in a new direction, casting architectural sculptures in concrete which she called 'sculpture by the yard'. Exhausted by the physical effort involved in this process, she took up teaching in London, New York and Montreal before succumbing to Alzheimer's.

Royal Academician Stephen Farthing was convinced that Cunliffe had been overlooked by an establishment not 'interested in a female American artist making sculpture in a garage in Didsbury'. He felt she deserved to be ranked alongside Jackson Pollock and Barbara Hepworth and curated an exhibition of her work in Oxford in 1994. In 2016, Leeds University repeated the tribute, with 'Sculptor behind the Mask', an exhibition celebrating the 60th anniversary of her *Man-Made Fibres* sculpture.

GARSTANG'S MUMMY

Flashes from the archives of oblivion

*Garstang Museum, 14 Abercromby Square, University of Liverpool Campus,
L69 7WZ
www.liverpool.ac.uk/archaeology-classics-and-egyptology/garstang-museum/
Open for guided tours by appointment only on 0151 794 6793 or garstang@liv.
ac.uk
Any bus to the campus
15-min walk up Brownlow Hill from Central or Lime Street station*

Tucked away off Abercromby Square behind one of the few surviving
hexagonal Victorian letter boxes (see page 76) is a hidden treasure
trove of archaeological delights. Known as the Garstang Museum, it
is named after John Garstang, founder of the university's Archaeology
Department in 1904. Heavily involved with excavations across Egypt,
Sudan and the Near East, he pioneered the use of photography to record
the finds and was involved in archaeological schools in Sudan, Jerusalem
and Ankara. On the centenary of the Institute at Liverpool, the museum
was officially renamed in his honour.

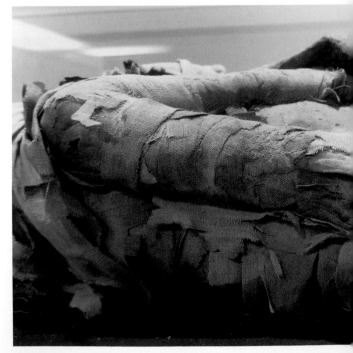

To coincide with this celebration, the 'Garstang mummy' was returned to the museum following 74 years in the Department of Anatomy. During its time there, it became one of the first mummies to undergo X-ray investigation. This revealed a man who 'was in his late 20s when he died ... He lived well, and was likely a member of the elite section of society – this is reflected in the good condition of his teeth.' He was used to trial the scientific techniques adopted in examining the royal remains of Tutankhamun.

Also on display is one of Garstang's first exhibits: the beautifully decorated coffin of Userhat. At each corner stands a canopic jar containing the soldier's organs, each protected by a different god.

Unfortunately, Garstang's greatest discovery (the Meroë Head) was kidnapped by the British Museum and features in Neil MacGregor's wonderful *A History of the World in 100 Objects*. It is a rare bronze of Augustus (first Roman emperor and later a god). The museum has other relics from ancient Greece and Rome but pride of place is given to those North African civilisations from which Europe learned so much ... and which challenge the Greek Tourist Board's oft-repeated claim that Crete is 'the cradle of civilisation'.

Jolly Posties on Parade - Liverpool's rarest letter boxes

When he wasn't writing novels or giving literary talks at the Liverpool Mechanics' Institute, Anthony Trollope worked for the Post Office. To cope with the increased volume of postage following postal reform in 1840, he introduced a 'letter-receiving pillar'. To the untrained eye, pillar boxes may appear to be a mundane feature of the cultural landscape, but every one has its own unique key and they come in a variety of designs (as many as 600). Each box also bears the Royal Cipher, indicating who was on the throne at the time of its casting. Some are rarer than others, fetching ridiculous prices on the black market, especially among rogue collectors in Russia, the US and the Far East ... so keep a watchful eye on your local one. There are said to be 14 rare Victorian models across the city, with the cast iron, hexagonal Penfold pillar box at the junction of Abercromby Square and Chatham Street (L69 7WZ) taking pride of place following its disappearance a few years back. After much sleuthing on behalf of the Letter Box Study Group (LBSG), it was discovered in bits on university premises following a collision with a truck. It has now been fully restored with 'cornice, pellet moulding and petal ogival cap with acorn finial' all back in the right sequence. Just don't try to post a letter as it's no longer in service.

The 'Liverpool Special' (officially classified by the LBSG as Box 1049678, a PB1005/2), which celebrated its 150th birthday in 2013, was created on the insistence of the Liverpool Postmaster. Complaining that the standard boxes were 'not adequate to cope with the heavy postings experienced in Liverpool, where (unlike London) the posting of newspapers as well as letters was permitted', he came up with his own design for a larger-capacity pillar box. Only seven of this design (unique to Liverpool) were ever made, of which three survive. The only one in operation can be found at the Albert Dock (Salthouse Quay, L3 4AN0) to where it was moved from Sheil Road in 1990. One languishes behind closed doors in the North Liverpool delivery office while the other is on public display at the Postal Museum in Essex. The other four have disappeared altogether. Several post boxes were cast during the reign of Edward VIII, uncrowned monarch for less than a year. Consequently, only 161 were ever made, some of which have been stolen or vandalised. Of those that remain, three survive in Liverpool. This one graces the corner of Bedford Street (L7 7BT).

Last, and most definitely least, is the kiddies' model made especially for the Fazakerley Children's Home. This was rescued by postie Harry Mac (founder member of the LBSG), when the home closed in 1964 and child-care organisations were invited to offer the unique miniature a new home. Such was the demand from around the country that the post box was donated instead to the Museum of Liverpool, where it can still be seen.

PHILHARMONIC PUB URINALS

Stand and Deliver!

36 Hope Street, L1 9BX
0151 707 2837
www.nicholsonspubs.co.uk/restaurants/northwest/
thephilharmonicdiningroomsliverpool
Mon–Sat 11am–midnight, Sun 11am–11pm
Central station or any bus to Hardman Street

Out-of-towner or local, tourist or tippler, there can be few visitors who have not admired the decor of the 'Phil'. Inside and out, it is England's most ornate pub. But few people – and probably only the very occasional lady – have appreciated the true value of its Gents.

Designed by Walter W. Thomas, the Gents was built for brewer Robert Cain whose proclaimed purpose was 'to beautify (his) public houses' and challenge the prejudices of the Temperance movement – if working men insisted on spending their wages on drink, they should at least enjoy the comforts and benefits of a pseudo-classical culture ... and the Gents was no exception.

According to Twyford's, 'The door has two deep etched panels and inside are the original 1890's Rouge Royale by Twyford's – five red marble urinals, three luxurious washbasins, glinting mosaic floor and original gleaming brass fittings, coloured tiles in relief on the walls and oblong bevelled mirror in tiled surround – also a mosaic panel under the Adamant cistern.'

Although the Gents is hidden from 50% of the population, women can sneak an escorted peek by arrangement ... although it has been known for the odd impatient feminist to nip in when the coast is clear. They need not tarry in the Ladies for, we are reliably informed, this would be a great disappointment – it is only what it was intended to be: a bog-standard afterthought.

In 1978, Lucinda Lambton's *Temples of Convenience* (about the heritage of Britain's public lavatories) was inspired by 'the particularly magnificent red "marble" urinals – agleam with cut glass, mosaic and mahogany – in the Gents of The Philharmonic Pub in Liverpool ... It was then that I realised the full wacky extent of Britain's 19th-century sanitary splendour.'

On UN World Toilet Day (19 November 2015), the Gents at the Phil was acclaimed the best in Liverpool.

Legends of pop

At the height of his fame, John Lennon is alleged to have lamented: 'The price of fame is not being able to go to the Phil for a quiet pint.' However, there is no truth in the rumour that Adam Ant took his name from the cistern above the urinal.

MICK JONES' MURAL

The lost art of protest

<u>Hope Street Hotel,</u> *40 Hope St, L1 9DA*
0151 709 3000
www.hopestreethotel.co.uk
Central station and 15-min from Lime Street or any busses stopping on
Hardman Street or Berry Street

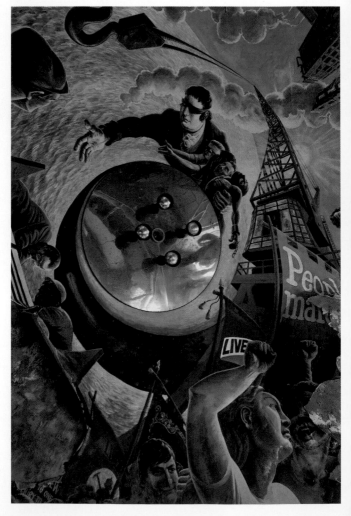

Hidden from public view on a staircase behind the reception area of Hope Street's boutique hotel, and thought by many to have disappeared altogether, is a partially restored mural recalling a more conflicted political age.

Originally painted inside the cupola of the Merseyside Trade Union Centre on Hardman Street in 1986 by Mick Jones, the son of trade union leader Jack Jones, this mural dominated the stairwell until the centre was closed in 2004. Jones' work depicts general struggles and working-class heroes, but the whole piece is dominated by the blind poet and radical campaigner Edward Rushton.

Whether or not you approve of propaganda as an art form or socialist realism as a style, this example was always hard to ignore and is fondly remembered by many. But memories fade and so did this neglected call to arms as rain seeped through the roof and gradually wore away the fragile paintwork behind closed doors. The venue was reopened during the Liverpool Biennial in 2014 to house an exhibition of 'impenetrable art installations', which paled by comparison with the fading mural above. This sparked a short and ultimately fruitless discussion about the future of the work among left-leaning enthusiasts. In the end, the intervention of private business seems to have saved Mick's radical alternative to the Sistine Chapel.

When the centre was purchased by Dave Brewitt, many feared the worst, but he has committed to restoring as much of the mural as possible. According to the hotel's creative director, Mary Colston, about two-thirds can be saved. 'Once we make it into an Italian fresco,' she assures me, 'it will look a lot better.'

The refurbished mural will not be on general public display, but hotel residents, diners and genuine enthusiasts are welcome to request a peek (contact Reception).

Mick Jones won a scholarship to the Birmingham School of Art and was inspired by his visits to Czechoslovakia and Mexico. He shared the politics of his father and placed his talents at the service of the labour movement. Many examples of his work survive, such as the Fitzrovia Mural in Camden and (in better repair) *Unemployment on Merseyside* in the Museum of Liverpool. He died of cancer in 2012.

THE FLY IN THE LOAF'S COAT OF ARMS

A forgotten past as Liverpool's most prestigious bakery

13 Hardman Street, L1 9AS
Central or Lime Street station, or any bus to Hardman Street or Berry Street

Today 'the Fly' is a popular real ale pub that retains its original tiling in the doorway. A coat of arms above indicates its forgotten past as the most prestigious bakery in Liverpool. Over the centuries, the Royal Warrant has been awarded to tradespeople serving royal households – in this case, the Kirkland brothers were probably being recognised by Queen Victoria for supplying biccies and butties to the Emperor of Austria, the King of Spain and Victoria herself.

The bakery began life in 1888 as Kirkland's Vienna Bakery. Purpose built by Henry Hartley with tiling by Stubbs & Son, the new premises had a double-filter water system that made it 'one of the finest (bakeries) in England'. Under later management, the Royal Arms were covered up but, when it reopened as Kirkland's Cafe Bar in the 1970s, the signage was restored. It became Liverpool's first Cafe Society experiment with a wine bar/pavement cafe and a nightclub upstairs hosting local bands such as Frankie Goes to Hollywood and Deaf School. In a benefit for the

Lyceum in 1978, Julian Cope and Ian McCulloch formed a one-gig-only band (Ugh?) before going on to form The Teardrop Explodes and Echo & the Bunnymen respectively.

The Fly was refurbished by Okell's Brewery in 2003.

The legend behind the pub's name

The legend behind the pub's name derives from the Old Testament story of Joseph interpreting the dreams of a butler and a baker imprisoned by the Pharaoh. Genesis does not reveal the causes of the Pharaoh's displeasure but the Midrashic tradition suggests that the butler presented the boss with a cup of wine into which a kamikaze fly had crash-landed, while the baker had carelessly allowed a stone to get into the loaf.

At some point this gets lost in translation and (in the 1886 version) the pebble is confused with the fly, the butler pays the ultimate price and Kirkland's adopted the wrong slogan. Following a recent £150K refit, the owners are in no mood to rebrand the pub.

Health Warning for all bar staff

In ancient Babylon, the penalty for serving a short measure was death by drowning.

MACKENZIE'S PYRAMID

A very tall story

St Andrew's Place
Rodney Street, L1 9ED
10-min walk from Central or Lime Street station or by bus to Hardman Street

Among the gravestones in St Andrew's Place on Rodney Street sits a tall granite pyramid marking the resting place of James MacKenzie. A millionaire who made a fortune excavating the Edge Lane to Lime Street tunnel and building railways across Europe, MacKenzie made another fortune as a successful gambler. To mark his time on earth, he had himself interred sitting up and clutching an unbeatable hand.

This is not unheard of – the Chinese often honour the passing of an ancestor who was partial to a bit of a flutter by burying him (or her) with fake money and papier mâché items to bring luck at the big casino in the sky. What makes this more than simply the eccentric whim of a wealthy atheist buried in the grounds of a Scottish Presbyterian church is that MacKenzie may have been hedging his bets one last time.

According to the redoubtable Tom Slemen, local chronicler of all things ghoulish, MacKenzie's success was based upon a pact with Beelzebub. The story involves ghostly apparitions in Rodney Street and a card game in which MacKenzie wagers his soul with a sinister out-of-towner called Madison. After winning the final hand, Madison reveals himself to be the devil in disguise and departs with the following words: 'Fear not, vain and defeated one. I will not take your soul until you are laid to rest in your grave.'

Determined to cheat Satan of the ultimate prize, MacKenzie insists on being entombed above ground in an upright position. Thus freed from an eternity in Hell, his ghost is condemned to roam the local streets in penance for his apostasy. Should you spend a bit too long in the eponymous whiskey bar on the corner of Rodney Street, you may well bump into him in your search for a cab.

However, on closer inspection, the tomb's inscription gives the game away: 'In the vault beneath lie the remains of William MacKenzie of Newbie Dumfrishire, Esquire who died 29th October 1851 aged 57 years (along with the remains of his two wives) ... This monument was erected by his Brother Edward as a token of love and affection A.D. 1868. The memory of the just is blessed.' As MacKenzie's second wife survived him by 15 years and the pyramid was not erected until the following year, the story sounds as tall as the pyramid itself.

STATUE OF WILLIAM HUSKISSON

Desperately Seeking William, the world's first reported railway casualty

Dukes Terrace (off Duke Street), L1 4JS
10- min walk from Central station and the Liverpool One bus station

There are three statues commemorating the life of statesman, financier and member of parliament William Huskisson, and none of them resides in the mausoleum constructed for that purpose: a visit to the vault in St James' cemetery reveals an empty plinth, a few fag packets and a deflated football. Considering that Huskisson was killed by Stephenson's Rocket, it is perhaps appropriate that the world's first reported railway casualty should be commemorated by a structure that resembles a sandstone spaceship ... but where is he hiding?

On the fateful day, 15 September 1830, Huskisson was one of the party celebrating the opening of the Liverpool to Manchester railway as guests of the prime minister, the Duke of Wellington. At Parkway they paused to take on water and Huskisson made the mistake of paying the Duke a visit. In confused circumstances, he fell beneath the oncoming Rocket and was badly mangled. At the breakneck speed of 38 mph, Stephenson rushed him on the Northumbrian to Eccles, where he survived long enough to make his will. The survivors continued on to Manchester, where the locals (not yet familiar with delays) met their PM with a volley of rotten vegetables and Lancastrian abuse.

The Liverpool MP was buried with much pomp and a marble statue was erected to mark the spot within a gated mausoleum ... much to the annoyance of members of the public, who failed to see the point of a three-dimensional structure that could only be admired from the front. To silence her critics, Mrs Huskisson had a replica made in bronze to adorn the Custom House. A third statue was commissioned and spent the next century keeping an eye on locals enjoying a stroll along Princes Avenue.

Three statues should be enough to honour the memory of any man (although Wellington has at least 22, and one for his horse) but where are they now?

The original suffered from industrial pollution, vandalism and bird muck and was removed to Liverpool Museum for renovation. Partly restored, it now resides within the Conservation Centre as a demonstration model. The second has ended up in Pimlico (south-west London) for no apparent reason. The third was hauled down by over-zealous protesters during the Toxteth riots of 1981 in the mistaken belief that Huskisson had been a slave trader. Now restored, he is to be found in the forecourt of the Dukes Terrace housing development.

Should you ever find yourself in Newton-le-Willows (midway between Liverpool and Manchester), a plaque marks the spot where Huskisson was killed nearly 190 years ago.

THE HARDMANS' HOUSE

Lifting the shutters

59 Rodney Street, L1 9ER (ticket office at rear on Pilgrim Street)
0151 709 6261
www.nationaltrust.org.uk/hardmans-house
March–October, Wed–Sat 11am–3.30pm, tour lasting approx. 90 mins (pre-booking recommended)
10-min walk from Central station and 5-min from bus stops on Hardman Street
Car parking available in 'Pay & Display' on Pilgrim Street or at the Anglican Cathedral

In the era of iPhone cameras and Photoshop, the painstaking and largely forgotten process involved in film photography is a thing of the past. However, the Hardmans' House, on Liverpool's premier Georgian street, is 'the only known British example of an intact 20th-century photographic studio' and celebrates the work of one of the county's greatest pictorial artists. This is a 'must-see' visit for any pre-digital photography enthusiast but is surely of interest to anyone with a hint of curiosity.

E. Chambré Hardman and his wife Margaret moved here from their studio on Bold Street in 1943 and lived out their lives in the place until 1988, when Hardman (now a widower and in the care of Social Services) died, leaving a massive archive and the house in the hands of trustees. The archive was destined for the Bradford National Science and Media Museum when the National Trust stepped in and arranged for it to be housed by the Central Library. A grant from the Heritage Lottery ensured that the Hardmans' home was preserved as a post-war time capsule complete with awful 1940s tiled fireplaces, period furniture and a kitchen bursting with rationed foodstuffs, a bottle of Graham's Golden Lager (rebranded as Skol in the 1960s) and a miniature drum of 'It foams as it cleans' Ajax.

Charging 5 guineas for 'a sitting plus two finished portraits', the Hardmans were in a league of their own as commercial photographers (the standard rate for a family snapshot at a high street photographer's was 2/6d). National celebrities and well-heeled Liverpolitans were their livelihood but, in their free time, they documented life on the streets of Liverpool and indulged a passion for the 'visionary power' of landscapes.

From the waiting room to the studio, dark room and touching-up desk, the house is more than a nostalgic celebration; it is a recreation of the process by which light was transformed into imagery in the era of film photography. Each step of the laborious process is featured in the layout of the house and every floor is decorated with examples of the Hardmans' work, letters of appreciation (and complaint) and reminders of their lives together over the shop. The exhibition room contains some wonderful examples of his work and highlights a current project developing films which never made it to the darkroom.

The archive has been given a digital update and can be viewed on the National Trust website. For those seeking an analogue experience, it is possible to make an appointment with the Central Library to view the real thing.

SECECRETS OF THE ANGLICAN CATHEDRAL

15

'Seek the city where I have sent you ... and pray to the Lord on its behalf'

St James Mount, L1 7AZ
www.liverpoolcathedral.org.uk
Daily, 8am–6pm
10-min walk from Central station or Liverpool One bus station

Towering above the old quarry of Mount Sion, the fifth-largest cathedral in the world contains hidden corners to explore and significant artefacts that are easy to miss in the overwhelming majesty of the place.

Tucked away behind the south choir aisle is the Lady Chapel – this was the first part of the jigsaw to be put in place and is accessed by a narrow flight of stairs. The stained-glass windows on the north and south sides commemorate the lives of holy women and saints, while those on the west wall are portraits of 'Noble Women' from the modern era, including Agnes Elizabeth Jones (the first trained Nursing Superintendent of Liverpool Workhouse Infirmary) and Kitty Wilkinson, who set up public wash houses and is buried in St James cemetery. The altar boasts a 15th-century carving of the *Kneeling Madonna* by Giovanni Della Robbia with an infant Christ added by Don McKinlay in 2002.

Return to the aisle and, directly opposite the stairs, is the memorial to David Sheppard, bishop of Liverpool from 1975 to 1979 and the only ordained minister to have played Test cricket. The naturally shaped stone sculpture is embedded into the etched stonework to create a rippling effect symbolising Sheppard's impact on the city (see photo).

Nearby is the tomb of Frederick Stanley, 16th Earl of Derby. (Stanley Park is named after him as is the cup he donated to Canada's national sport.) Search for the 'church mouse' keeping him company. It is thought that the humble mouse is there to remind us that 'all creatures (great or small) are welcome in God's house'.

A trip up the tower includes the Elizabeth Hoare Gallery but, if ecclesiastical embroidery is not your thing, then go for the views from the gallery overlooking the great open space provided for in Gilbert Scott's redesign. A scary ascent of the belfry stairs allows a peek at the Bartlett Bells. Continue to the very top and spot Scott's initials on the north-west pinnacle (dated 1942). Scott claimed to have only ever designed a pipe rack before planning the cathedral, but he also found time to design the iconic red telephone box: 20,000 K6s were installed throughout the UK during the 1930s and one stands guard at the tower entrance.

Not content with the highest and heaviest peal of bells in the world, the cathedral also has the 'largest musical instrument ever conceived': the Grand Organ has 10,268 pipes and you can adopt one as part of its renovation appeal.

On your way out, say goodbye to Tracy Emin's *For You*, her attempt to have us contemplate 'feelings of love' which is mounted above the West Doors.

As a Catholic, Scott was buried with his wife outside his masterpiece. His grave, obscured for years beneath the entrance to the car park, was restored in 2012. Secretly buried in the foundations is a time capsule from socialist stonemason Fred Bower in which he lamented, 'Within a stone's throw from here, human beings are housed in slums not fit for swine.'

THE OUROBOROS AND THE BUTTERFLY

16

'To infinity and beyond'

St James' Garden, L1 7AZ
www.stjamescemetery.co.uk
All year, 24/7
10 -min walk from Central station or Liverpool One bus station

Between the Anglican Cathedral and the Oratory lies a spooky passageway hewn from solid rock and lined with headstones. Originally a quarry for stone used in the construction of the docks, the

old Corn Exchange and the Town Hall during the 18th century, it was subsequently redesigned as a graveyard to cope with overspill from the Liverpool Necropolis on Low Hill. Complete with ramps, catacombs, an oratory and a porter's lodge, it became the final resting place for Liverpolitans (in family vaults) and a multitude of paupers (in communal pits).

Directly opposite the tunnel's exit into the cemetery are a group of obelisks in the middle of which is the tomb of William Taylor Barry, newly appointed as American ambassador to Madrid. He never made it and died in Liverpool en route in 1835. Take a closer look at the symbols on the gravestone to find an ouroboros symbolising eternal life encircling a butterfly representing resurrection. The icon of a serpent eating its own tail goes back to Ancient Egypt and crops up across the centuries in alchemy, Gnosticism, Norse mythology and Freemasonry. It occasionally appears on Victorian tombstones (see page 96 for more information on the ouroboros). The butterfly was less widely used but a combination of the two is very rare.

Opened for business on 11 June 1829, the first interment at St James was accompanied by the worst thunderstorm in living memory. By the 20th century, this 'vast stone forest of memory' had reached bursting point, with a silent congregation of almost 60,000. It finally shut up shop in 1936 and was landscaped as a park. Consequently, the headstones were repositioned in the walls of the park while their owners slumber on beneath the trees (see following double-page spread).

Long neglected, the park became the established venue for hard drugs and casual sex (used condoms were often displayed as trophies on the branches of trees). But the Friends of St James turned it around by ridding the place of its detritus and planting hundreds of wild flowers. It is now a haven of tranquillity beneath the city's many enjoyed by rabbits, squirrels, blackbirds, jays and a community of local dog walkers. It features a Chalybeate spring that was claimed to cure 'the colic, the melancholy, and the vapours; it made the lean fat, the fat lean; it killed flat worms in the belly, loosened the clammy humours of the body, and dried the over-moist brain.'

It can be sad to read some of the inscriptions, especially those of children from the Orphan Asylums and the Blue Coat Hospital but this is not a maudlin place. Alongside the dead – and sometimes right on top of them – locals walk their dogs and schoolkids play among the headstones. The park even hosts the occasional Shakespeare play. If you get the chance and the weather is good, bring a picnic and enjoy an al fresco performance of *A Midsummer Night's Dream*.

For more information about St James' cemetery, please see following double pages.

Dormitory of the dead

The roll call at St James' cemetery includes many celebrities and one or two graves that simply inspire curiosity. Close to **Huskisson's** vacant tomb (see page 88) is the grave of architect **John Foster Jnr**. Despite being dismissed by his colleague Charles Cockerell as 'a most amusing youth, but too idle to be anything more than a dinner companion', Foster played a major role in the creation of 19th-century Liverpool. His works include designing the cemetery and its Oratory; Gambier Terrace; St Luke's Church (widely known

as 'the Bombed-Out Church'); and St Andrew's on Rodney Street. Close by lie the remains of Edward Rushton (see page 81) and **Kitty Wilkinson** – founder of the public wash house and in her own way just as important to the city's development.

Adjacent to the tunnelled entrance lies **Captain Elisha Lindsay Halsey**, an American sea captain who, in 1844, met an 'untimely death' at the hands of the ship's Liverpudlian cook. Attempts to have the cook extradited to stand trial in America were thwarted and he was acquitted on grounds of 'justifiable homicide'.

The **Keay brothers** perished on different legs of the triangular trade ... some twenty years after the abolition of the slave trade! Meanwhile the **De la Cruz family** headstone reminds us that many Filipinos made their homes in Liverpool – Greenland Street and Upper Frederick Street formed a hub known as 'Little Manila'. One stone records the dying wish of 9-year-old **Eliza Clements**, who passed away in San Francisco in 1865: 'At her request, her remains were brought here by her bereaved parents and interred near the "old home".'

'Little Grace' is a mystery: just a name on a stone in the wall to the left of the spring, but executed with some skill.

Two you will never find

Thanks to those responsible for 'improvements' in the 1970s, several significant headstones have disappeared.

- **Sarah Biffen:** born with vestigial legs and no arms, Sarah measured 37 inches and spent several years as the 'Limbless Wonder' in a freak show where she painted portraits using her mouth. Rescued by the Earl of Morton, she was accepted by the Royal Academy and awarded a medal by the Society of Artists in 1821. She is mentioned in works by Dickens and Thackeray but, despite royal patronage and a pension from William IV, she died in poverty. A self-portrait from the 1840s was recently valued on The Antiques Roadshow at between £3,000 and £4,000.

- **Captain John Oliver:** born in Tavistock in 1774, Oliver ran away to sea at the age of 10 and was press-ganged into the navy at 20. He served with Nelson on HMS *Victory* at Trafalgar but deserted after the war and joined the merchant navy, retiring at the age of 85. He died at Northumberland Street aged 102.

Use the website's database to track down individual headstones.

The Ouroboros: a symbol of divine illumination

The figure of a coiled serpent biting its own tail is sometimes found in iconography and literature. This symbol is traditionally known as the *Ouroboros* or *Uroboros*, a Greek word derived from the Coptic and Hebrew languages – *ouro* is Coptic for "king" and *ob* Hebrew for "serpent" – meaning "royal serpent". Thus the reptile raising its head above its body is used as a symbol of mystical illumination: for Eastern peoples, it represents the divine fire they call Kundalini. Kundalini is the origin of the association that Western medicine of the Middle Ages and Renaissance made between, on the one hand, the body heat that rises from the base of the spine to the top of the head and, on the other, the *venena bibas* ("ingested venom" mentioned by Saint Benedict of Nursia) of the snake whose bite can only be treated by an equally potent poison. Just as the Eastern techniques of spiritual awakening, Dzogchen and Mahamudra, show how a meditating person must learn to "bite his tail like the serpent", the theme of the *Ouroboros* and ingested venom is a reminder that spiritual awareness can only result from a devout life: by elevating your consciousness onto a mental plane surpassing the ordinary, you search within to truly find yourself as an eternal being. The Greeks popularised the word ouroboros in its literal sense of "serpent biting its tail". They acquired this image from the Phoenicians through contact with the Hebrews, who had themselves adopted it from Egypt where the Ouroboros featured on a stele dated as early as 1600 BC. There it represented the sun god Ra (Light), who resurrects life from the darkness of the night (synonymous with death), going back to the theme of eternal return, life, death, and the renewal of existence, as well as the reincarnation of souls in successive human bodies until they have reached their evolutionary peak, which will leave them perfect, both physically and spiritually – a theme dear to Eastern peoples.

In this sense, the serpent swallowing itself can also be interpreted as an interruption of the cycle of human development (represented by the serpent) in order to enter the cycle of spiritual evolution (represented by the circle).

Pythagoras associated the serpent with the mathematical concept of infinity, coiled up as zero – the abstract number used to denote eternity, which becomes reality when the *Ouroboros* is depicted turning around on itself.

Gnostic Christians identified it with the Holy Spirit revealed through wisdom to be the Creator of all things visible and invisible, and whose ultimate expression on Earth is Christ. For this reason, the symbol is associated in Greek Gnostic literature with the phrase *hen to pan* (The All is One); it was commonly adopted in the 4th and 5th centuries as a protective amulet against evil spirits and veno-mous snakebites. This amulet was known as Abraxas, the name of a god in the original Gnostic pantheon that the Egyptians recognised as Serapis. It became one of the most famous magical talismans of the Middle Ages.

Greek alchemists very quickly espoused the figure of the *Ouroboros* and so it reached the Hermetic philosophers of Alexandria – among them, Arab thinkers who studied and disseminated this image in their schools of Hermeticism and alchemy.

These schools were known and sought out by medieval Christians. There is even historical evidence that members of the Order of the Knights Templar, as well as other Christian mystics, travelled to Cairo, Syria and even Jerusalem to be initiated into the Hermetic sciences.

ERIC HARALD MACBETH ROBERTSON'S MURALS

Liverpool's Moon Under Water

Peter Kavanagh's pub
2-6 Egerton St, L8 7LY
0151 709 3443
15-min walk from Central station and 20-min from Lime Street
Any bus to Catharine Street

An authentic pub in an atmospheric Victorian terrace on the edge of the 'Georgian Quarter', Peter Kavanagh's boasts walls in the front and back rooms (either side of the server) that are daubed with scenes from Dickens and Hogarth by the Scottish artist Eric Harald Macbeth Robertson: a little known feature the locals are proud to extol.

Influenced by the Pre-Raphaelites and French Symbolism, Robertson was hailed as 'one of the most creative and brilliant young artists of his day'. He married fellow artist Cecile Walton and together with Dorothy Johnstone they formed the Edinburgh Group. Any likely success was destroyed by Robertson's excessive drinking; Cecile moved in with Dorothy and Eric moved out ... to Liverpool. During the post war period, he flirted with abstract art (Vorticism) and has a depiction of the Anglican Cathedral in the Museum of Liverpool (it is hard to tell if this is a completed painting of the unfinished cathedral or if he just ran out of paint).

Rumour has it that the murals were in part payment of Eric's gargantuan bar bill, but it is more likely that he was commissioned to paint them by Kavanagh, who took great pleasure in converting Ma Bowman's old 'grog shop' into a retreat fit for gentlemen with wooden carvings around the walls, tables with specially-devised water-filled ash trays, ornate tiling work and a north-facing bay window cunningly devised to repel any hint of sunshine. The pub still retains most of the features Orwell required for the perfect city pub; 'only two minutes away from a bus stop, on a side street, consisting mainly of 'regulars' ... Uncompromisingly Victorian ... everything has the solid, comfortable ugliness of the nineteenth century ... with draught stout, open fires, cheap meals, a garden, motherly barmaids and no radio'.

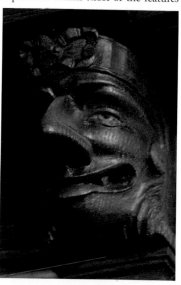

Over the years any 'comfortable ugliness' has been softened and, in some areas, completely obscured by a variety of artefacts which give the impression of a pub designed by Tracy Emin and Albert Steptoe.

Way back when

In the 1980s, Frank Milner, then at the Walker Art Gallery and a pub local, tells the story of a tipsy customer offering to restore the murals with a good scrubbing. Being the right person to have in the right place at the right time, Frank overheard the drunken blathering and intervened, pointing out that the work was water based and could not survive the proposed 'ordeal by Ajax'.

PRINCES ROAD SYNAGOGUE

'One of the finest examples of Orientalism in British synagogue architecture'

Liverpool Old Hebrew Congregation, Synagogue Chambers, Princes Road, L8 1TG
www.princesroad.org
Tours may be booked online. Free during Heritage Open Days
Any bus to Princes Road/Avenue or a hefty 25-min walk from the Central or Lime Street station

For one of the oldest Jewish communities in the UK, only the very best will do and the Princes Road Synagogue, in Moorish Revival style, is a Grade I Listed treasure. Described by the Liverpool Pevsner Architectural Guide as 'one of the finest examples of Orientalism in

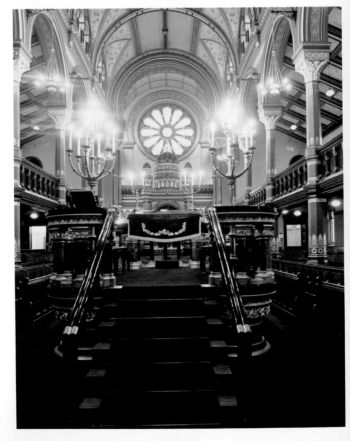

British synagogue architecture', its exterior hardly stands out against the surrounding red brick and stone buildings or the Greek Church of St Nicholas opposite – possibly due to the removal of its six minarets in the 1960s – but step inside and have the breath knocked out of your body.

The Star of David patterns by Minton in the entrance are a mere taster for what lies behind the giant doors: Moorish arches supported by green columns decorated with gold leaf that turn out to be made of cast iron (give one a gentle knock); and an Ark containing the Torah topped off with five Byzantine domes, all within the embrace of a horseshoe arch illuminated by a Gothic rose window. Abstract patterns, stars and stained-glass flora express the rejection of idolatry shared with many religions. An arson attack in 1979 destroyed the Ark. Luckily for us, the interior has now been restored to its former glory.

The earliest mention of Jewish settlement in Liverpool dates from 1753, when a synagogue was recorded on Cumberland Street (commemorated by a plaque in the Met Quarter). A second Jewish community, with no known links to the former, then appears in the 1780s; they worshipped first in Turton Court and then in Upper Frederick Street before moving to a purpose-built synagogue on Seel Street. (A plaque marks the spot on the rear end of a hideous building next door to the Pogue Mahone, home to the finest pint of Guinness in Liverpool.)

A breakaway group built a rival synagogue on Hope Place (now the Unity Theatre) but the Old Hebrew Congregation continued to grow and in 1872 laid the foundation stone for a grander home on Princes Avenue. Despite competition from six Jewish firms, the contract was won by Scottish Presbyterian brothers William and George Audsley, who had no experience of synagogues and hastily embarked on a Grand Tour of the world's best. This probably accounts for the heady combination of Byzantine, Gothic and Moorish influences.

The first-ever foreign-born Japanese consul

The Audsley brothers also built Streatlam Tower next door: an austere but imposing building erected for James Lord Bowes in the 1870s to accommodate his vast collection of Japanese art. His role as champion of Japanese culture was recognised by the Emperor, who appointed him as 'the first-ever foreign-born Japanese consul' in 1888. He was later awarded the Japanese Order of the Sacred Treasure. An exhibition of Japanese craft at the Tower attracted 20,000 visitors in six days and raised £5,290 (almost £600,000 in today's money), which was donated to charity.

ST PETER'S CHURCH

The 'Soul of Cuba'

Alma de Cuba cocktail bar, Seel Street, L1 4BH
www.alma-de-cuba.com
Gospel music Sun 12 noon–6pm
Central station or Liverpool One bus station

Before downing your third mojito in Alma de Cuba cocktail bar, take time to explore the nooks and crannies where religious artefacts act as clues to its past as Liverpool's oldest Catholic church.

When, in 2000, Urban Splash proposed the conversion into a boutique restaurant and cocktail bar, our neighbours were horrified. In 1957, they had been married in what was still their parish church and an enduring symbol of Catholic Emancipation.

The first Catholic church built in Liverpool following the Reformation was a chapel in Edmund Street, but this was destroyed in 1746 during a riot celebrating the defeat of the Jacobite Rebellion. A replacement was disguised as a warehouse and survived a similar attack in 1759. By the end of the century, restrictions on Catholic worship and education had been relaxed and St Peter's was built in 1788, although Catholic churches could not have steeples or bells to advertise their existence. This explains the simple brick structure with three galleries and king-post trusses supporting the barn-like roof – described by Sharples as 'virtually indistinguishable from a Methodist chapel'.

Given its symbolic significance, it is not surprising that the conversion into a cocktail bar (with its own secular 10 Commandments) and celebrating the 'Soul of Cuba' (a country where Catholicism was still repressed) sparked indignant opposition ... despite the fact that the building had been deconsecrated and was in danger of falling down. A compromise based on its listed status saw the retention of wooden panelling, memorial tablets, murals and stained-glass windows. The altar and pediment (dated 1898) feature a huge glass mirror to replace the portrait of St Peter that now resides in the Catholic Cathedral. The inscription has changed three times in the last century, 'Tu es Petrus' dating from the 1960s.

Every Sunday afternoon, a gospel choir provides a soulful winding down to the weekend.

A word of a caution before you order a Bombay Bad Boy or share a Zombie Barrel: during the Great Plague of 1847, Fr Appleton contracted typhus here and 'contrary to Doctor's orders he very injudiciously took some whiskey which acted like a poison on his constitution and terminated his life'. The year 1847 saw Dr Duncan's appointment as Britain's first Medical Officer of Health. A plaque on the Blue Angel at the top of the street marks his birthplace.

of the former Yamen Cafe

St, L1 4EZ
thisisleaf.co.uk/liverpool/contact/
Sun & Mon 9am–10pm, Tues & Wed 9am–11pm, Thurs 9am–12 midnight,
Fri & Sat 9am–late
Central station, Liverpool One bus station or any downtown bus

The fabulous art deco façade of the LEAF tea shop has a distinctive zigzag pattern with a tale to tell: the motif is in fact a repeat of the initials of William Watson (champion cyclist and racing driver), who gave the façade its 1930s make-over when he converted the ground floor into a Rolls Royce showroom. The 19th-century building started life as a chapel before becoming an Entertainment Hall, an Opera House and eventually ground-floor shops with the Yamen Cafe upstairs (see box).

Bold Street was originally one of the many 'ropewalks' servicing the port, but by the 19th century had become a residential street with a Music Hall and the Lyceum gentleman's club. It soon transformed itself into Liverpool's 'imperial trading street'. Known as 'the Bond Street of the North', it was the spot to indulge in a bit of Edwardian retail therapy, for those with the dosh and the desire to flaunt it.

In the late 1930s, Bold Street was still the affluent centre of gravity for wealthy consumers, but after the war it fell from favour, becoming the home of charity shops and bargain basements. The cafe made way for Coopers Food Hall while anyone interested in a Rolls Royce was compelled to visit Knutsford.

Since the Noughties, the street has enjoyed a revival, with a variety of ethnic restaurants, not forgetting the wonderful Matta's International Food Store for people who prefer to cook their own (www.mattas.co.uk). As part of this transformation, LEAF bought No. 65–67 and engaged Total Reuse to create some sturdy 10-ft tables 'for eating off during the day and dancing on at night'. Using trestle tables salvaged from St Joseph's Seminary in Upholland and original floorboards from the Bold Street building, they came up with the solution that greets you on your arrival (please refrain from dancing during mealtimes).

Venture upstairs and you'll find what used to be the home of the Yamen Cafe. According to local historian Stephen Guy, it is believed to be Liverpool's first vegetarian restaurant. Contemporary photographs adorning the walls show that it has retained much of its late Victorian style despite its current reputation as a laid-back contemporary cafe, bar and music venue.

NEARBY
His Master's Voice

No. 92 (now Forbidden Planet) was the studio of little-known artist Francis Barraud, who was intrigued by his dog Nipper's fascination with the phonograph. This inspired the painting *His Master's Voice*, completed in London and offered to the Edison recording company, who rejected it ('Dogs don't listen to phonographs'). Barraud substituted a gramophone for the phonograph and sold his painting to The Gramophone Company instead. Adopted by EMI, RCA and JVC, it became the most famous trademark in the world.

ROSCOE MEMORIAL

*The little-known final resting place
of William Roscoe*

*Roscoe Gardens, Mount Pleasant, L3 5SD
Central or Lime Street station or any bus stop on Ranelagh Street or Brownlow
Hill*

Opposite the breathtakingly hideous Mount Pleasant car park are what remains of the graveyard of Renshaw Street Unitarian Chapel. Now a tranquil park, it is home to a little-known and rather lacklustre monument commemorating the life of one of Liverpool's most famous sons. As a Unitarian, William Roscoe would never have been commemorated with grand monuments, so it probably comes as a surprise to learn that he did not end up with his chums at the Ancient Chapel of Toxteth (see page 202) but has this as his final resting place.

Merchant banker, botanist, art collector, man of letters, political radical, abolitionist and all-round Renaissance Man (he even penned the much-loved children's verse *The Butterfly's Ball*), self-educated William Roscoe was inspired by the poetry and painting of the Italian Renaissance. He became, according to curator Xanthe Brooke, 'Liverpool's cultural

impresario, the city's leading art collector, and an internationally known biographer of Lorenzo de' Medici and Pope Leo X'.

Convinced that Liverpool could become 'the Florence of the North', Roscoe sponsored many educational and artistic establishments in the city, including the now defunct Academy of Arts, the Royal Institution at 24 Colquitt Street (now a lounge bar) and Liverpool's first Botanic Garden, which rivalled Kew but moved in 183 to the Botanical Gard off Edge Lane (remr still there).

Roscoe supported the French Revolution, the emancipation of women and Catholics and, most famously, in a city where 'every brick was cemented with an African's blood', the abolition of the slave trade. Nevertheless, as a merchant banker and a member of the Athenaeum, he found it difficult to avoid a degree of 'Liverpool taint': his business partner and political sponsor, Thomas Leyland, was a slave trader ... as was Thomas Earl, who supported his candidacy for parliament. In 1806, Roscoe was the first Liverpool MP ever to condemn the slave trade, but he also spoke in favour of compensating slave traders for their loss of livelihood.

Joseph Blanco White: a Spanish secret

Also buried here are the remains of Joseph Blanco White, much despised in his own country and until recently hidden from its history. A naturally curious free thinker, Blanco White was to discover that these are not the attributes cherished in a Spanish priest at the fag end of the Inquisition. He left for England branded as a heretic and a traitor due to his calls for constitutional reform at home and independence for Spain's dominions in the Americas. After conversion to Anglicanism and yet another ordination, he rejected the dogmatism of the established Church and joined like-minded Unitarians in Liverpool, where he died in 1841. In the post-Franco era, Blanco White's writings have found a new audience and his reputation has been restored. As part of this rehabilitation, a delegation from his home town, Seville, has unveiled a plaque to his memory beside Roscoe's.

The Roscoe Head pub

Roscoe was born at the summit of Mount Pleasant at the Old Bowling Green pub run by his parents (see page 70). Appropriately, on a street bearing his name, 'the Roscoe' is named in his honour but is due to be demolished to make way for a retail development. Get there while you still can.

5TH FLOOR AT THE LEWIS'S BUILDING

The floor the lift forgot

Aparthotel Adagio, 1 Fairclough Street, L1 1FS
0151 703 7400
Open to the public on Heritage Open Days and for hotel guests or by
appointment (email: h7332@adagio-city.com)
Any bus to Renshaw Street or Central station next door

Access to the famous Lewis's building via its infamous entrance is no longer possible: you will need to take a lift from the Aparthotel's reception to the breakfast bar where a real treat awaits. For locals of a certain vintage, the 5th Floor holds an iconic place in the memory as home to a cafeteria, two restaurants and a huge hairdressing salon. Some features survive, including a splendid 65-foot (20-metre) mural crafted from hand-painted (and printed) tiles commissioned from Carter & Co. of Poole and portraying kitchen utensils and foodstuffs. Etched wooden panelling, created by the Design Research Institute as a backdrop to the Mersey Rooms Restaurant, depicts over 600 years of local history.

Refurbished after the war and dedicated to the 'democratisation of luxury', Lewis's was the ultimate family firm, sometimes boasting three loyal generations of the same family in its workforce. After 150 years in the city, and powerless to resist the rationalisation of the retail sector and changes in shopping habits, it closed down floor by floor. It became the nucleus of the ill-fated Central Village development and is now in the hands of another developer; the building is currently home to the

Aparthotel Adagio, a 24-hour gym and a grim replacement for the much-missed Leece Street Post Office.

Whatever its future, Lewis's was always 'much more than a place to shop': ask for it by name and, even if the driver of the 82 bus never shopped there, he will know exactly where to drop you off. 'Meeting under Dickie Lewis' remains a widely understood idiomatic expression. Inquire after the Mersey Rooms or the Red Rose Restaurant, however, and you enter shakier territory.

Closed in the 1980s, the 5th Floor ended its days as 'a repository for a surreal collection of unwanted retail paraphernalia'. This became the subject of a quirky photographic study by Stephen King: in 2009, he turned the space into a temporary workshop and interviewed 40 past employees to help him make sense of it all.

The twisted mannequins, Diplomat hairdryers and outdated toys cluttering the place have long since departed, but listing of the building has meant that many of the original features and fittings remain. Unfortunately, Mitzi Cunliffe's bronze sculpted screen that once divided the Red Rose Restaurant was reclaimed by the artist and now resides in Florence (see page 72).

Memory lane

On Heritage Open Day 2017, an elderly couple turned up just to sit in the same spot they shared on their first date as 16-year-olds. 'We had our very first curry and chips here,' they said through the tears. 'You've made us so happy.'

SEFTON SUITE

Past links to the transatlantic liner trade

Britannia Adelphi Hotel, Ranelagh Place, L3 5UL
5-min walk from the Central or Lime Street station

Through the entrance hall of the Adelphi Hotel, steps lead to the impressive Central Court, the Hypostyle Hall beyond and the adjacent Sefton Suite, all of which recall the hotel's past links to the transatlantic liner trade. The decor reflects the splendour of lounges on board the *Titanic*; however, claims that the Sefton Suite is 'an exact replica of the First Class Smoking Lounge' are an exaggeration.

Acquired by Midland Railway Hotels in 1892, the Adelphi was replaced in 1914 by what turned out to be the last railhead city hotel ever constructed. 'The world's most palatial hotel', it combined the best of American style and English comfort with all the 'refinement of a Parisian salon', but the days of pampered travel were numbered. Under the stewardship of British Transport Hotels, the top two floors were abandoned to reduce costs and a period of steady decline followed (a 1997 fly-on-the-wall TV documentary, *Hotel*, probably marked its nadir).

A buy-out in 1982 saved the hotel from closure and a lengthy renovation by Britannia Hotels has seen it restored to something of its former glory. For many Liverpudlians it has been an enduring symbol of

social exclusion, but its Edwardian decor can be appreciated nowadays by anyone choosing to take afternoon tea in the Central Court lounge.

The Great and the not so Good …

In its time, the Adelphi has hosted the rich and the famous: Dickens was a regular, Winston Churchill and Harold Wilson roomed here. Roy Rogers paraded his four-legged friend Trigger on the hotel balcony during his 'Singing Cowboy' tour of 1954 and Dylan camped in a suite during the infamous 'Judas' tour in 1966. We can find no evidence, however, for the story that Hitler waited on tables, although there is a link to murdered fascist sympathiser Lord Erroll. In the 'Happy Valley' murder case, which scandalised wartime Nairobi, Sir "Jock" Delves Broughton was acquitted of killing Erroll following a dubious court case (later featured in the film *White Mischief*). Delves Broughton returned to Liverpool, where he committed suicide in his room at the Adelphi.

The current hotel had two predecessors. The one it replaced (aka 'the Second Adelphi') imported live green turtles from the Caribbean. They were pampered in steam-heated tanks in the basement until required for the world-renowned Adelphi turtle soup, 60 litres of which were distributed around the country for functions every day.

LIVERPOOL 800 PAINTING

It's a Singh Twin thing

St George's Hall Heritage Centre
St George's Place, L1 1JJ
www.singhtwins.co.uk
Lime Street station

Through a concealed entrance on St George's Place, and immediately to the right, is a small cafe which makes little fanfare of an extraordinary painting by twins Rabindra and Amrit Singh, hanging on the wall.

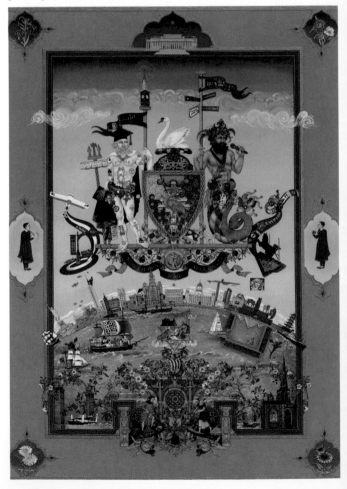

Called *Liverpool 800*, it was commissioned by the City Council and depicts eight centuries of Liverpool's heritage and identity through references to the sea, trade, education and popular culture in the twins' own distinctive miniaturist style.

Best described as 'Twindividuals', the Singhs share genes, kindred skills, a love of painting and a similar moral outlook (although one of them doesn't like blue cheese and the other adores it). They conduct joint research, share their discoveries and work together on the same canvases, often at the same time.

'We started off developing our individual work ... but, as time went on, we both wanted a joint input ...That does often involve sitting side-by-side and painting together, or we'll go head-to-head ... It can get a little difficult but mostly we manage not to injure each other with our paint brushes!'

Not only a different way of working, there is also the small matter of cultural preference. 'From the point of view of Sikh ... philosophy, the community comes first and the individual is second,' they say. This did not go down well with their tutors, who told them that their preoccupation with Indian miniaturist art was 'backward and outdated'. Things came to a head at Chester College when the external examiner downgraded their degree classification, leading to a four-year legal battle to clear their name.

Undeterred, the twins have eventually achieved the recognition they deserve: in 2002, they became the first British-born artists since Henry Moore to be exhibited at the New Delhi National Museum of Modern Art; in 2009, they were made Honorary Citizens of Liverpool; two years later, they received an MBE for 'Services to the Indian miniature tradition of painting within Contemporary Art', and in 2015, Chester University awarded them Honorary Doctorates for their 'outstanding contribution to British Art'.

Their 'Past-Modern' work has resulted in a celebration of their adopted home (*Liverpool 800;* and *Art Matters*: *The Pool of Life* at the Museum of Liverpool's Wondrous Place gallery); a condemnation of colonialism (*Slaves of Fashion,* scheduled for a world tour); and the satirical representation of Posh & Becks as the new Royal Family in *From Hero to Zero* (see their website).

The inspiration for *Liverpool 800* is explored in the animated DVD *The Making of Liverpool.*

ROAD PEACE MEMORIAL

The reality of road crashes

St John's Gardens, William Brown Street, L1 1JJ
0845 4500 355
www.roadpeace.org
5-min walk from Lime Street station or the Queen Square bus station

Among the memorials to Scousers lost to war in the oddly nicknamed 'Peace Garden' is a permanent memorial to those killed in traffic accidents. A bronze traffic bollard shaped like a miniature coffin is adorned with artefacts to remind us of lives cut short by the mayhem on our roads: a walking stick, a school bag, an abandoned teddy bear and a wristwatch forever stopped at five minutes to nine.

In place of the sad bouquets of floral tributes flapping from lampposts by a thread of Sellotape, Tom Murphy's statue provides an enduring tribute to the victims and a collective place of remembrance for bereaved families. Commissioned by Liverpool City Council in conjunction with the charity Road Peace, the statue also highlights the need for awareness (there are still five deaths a day on our roads) and Road Peace's campaign for improved safety, justice for victims and support for families left behind.

A World Remembrance Day service is held in nearby St George's Hall every year. It is followed by a vigil at the statue, where five doves are released to remind us there is still much to be done. Instrumental in this has been Pauline Fielding, a trustee of the charity and whose own son was killed 25 years ago in a hit and run (the driver was never traced). As Pauline says, 'In every death there are so many people affected and this service offers the families and friends of those who have died or been injured the opportunity to come together and remember their loved ones ... and reflect on what can be done to prevent further tragedies.'

A forgotten link between Liverpool and the Napoleonic Wars

Set into the curved wall at the top end of St John's Gardens, a plaque commemorates the hundreds of French POWs who died in appalling conditions in Liverpool Tower (Tower Buildings on Water Street marks the spot). They would have left no trace had it not been for the work of Dr James Currie. During Currie's time in Liverpool, the British were engaged in several wars with the French and countless skirmishes involving Liverpool privateers. This led to a good few French sailors ending up under lock and key. To while away their time and make some money, they crafted model ships and artworks – two examples can be found in the Victoria Gallery and Museum at the base of the staircase to the left of the Waterhouse Café. Conditions in Liverpool Tower were appalling and many prisoners starved to death. Currie campaigned successfully for improvements there that saved lives, but the dead POWs ended up in paupers' graves in the cemetery of St John's.

WILLIAM BROWN STREET FOSSILS

The building blocks of history

William Brown St, L3 8EW
www.liverpoolgeologicalsociety.org

Liverpool stands on layers of Triassic sandstone formed over 250 million years ago, but the city's architecture and infrastructure tell a much older story – not what Merseyside is made of, but what Liverpool is built from. To be sure, much of the sandstone used for civic buildings, churches and the early docks came from local quarries in Toxteth Park, St James Mount and Woolton (where 23,300 cubic metres of sandstone were extracted for the construction of the Anglican Cathedral alone). However, many of the city's cobbled streets, stone pavements and prestigious buildings used stone dating back over a billion years and imported from Scotland, Derbyshire and Scandinavia.

Within the granite from Finland or the stone from Darley Dale are tiny clues to the origins of the rock used to create a UNESCO-designated 'outstanding example of a world mercantile port city'. These are the fossils revealed when the great blocks of stone were cut to size – they remain in plain view beneath our feet. You can discover some of the finest examples in the vicinity of William Brown Street.

Firstly, there are the sedimentary structures created by tidal currents as the rock formed; these show up in the flagstones as patterns (casts or ripples) and are best viewed at the junction of Byron Street and William Brown Street and also on the steps of the Walker Art Gallery.

More extensive detective work will uncover 'trace fossils', the sedimentary record of animals going about their business and best seen in bright, low-angled sunlight. These denote the dwelling burrows, feeding traces and escape routes created by tiny prehistoric creatures.

The clearest example of a living burrow of a ragwort can be found on the pavement outside the Central Library, while the feeding burrow of a shrimp-like creature (known to his mates as Rhizocorallium) is on the pavement outside the double-doored side entrance adjacent to St George's Hall (directly opposite the Walker). This was hard to find, partly due to the sedimentary excavation necessary to remove the blob of Wrigley's gum gobbed on it by some local contemporary Neanderthal.

The fifth bollard facing the Steble Fountain has traces of a brachiopod and a wonderfully preserved colonial coral.

A fossil tree root (stigmaria) can be found five flags east of the turning circle outside the Library. The freshwater limestone on Boodles' shop front on Lord Street contains fossil snails, while the weathered walls of the Victoria Monument show fossils shells and corals.

Download the 'Rock around Liverpool' PDF from the LGS website (under Publications) for a detailed guide.

28

THE SECRETS OF WELLINGTON'S COLUMN

The lion's roar

Off William Brown Street, L3 8EL
5-min walk from Lime Street station or the Queen Square bus station

L iverpool has more statues than anywhere outside Westminster, and it's no surprise to find that the Duke of Wellington warrants one of them opposite the Walker Art Gallery. It is difficult to claim that a 40-metre-high column towering over the city centre is a 'secret' but the devil is in the detail: look closely and you'll notice a couple of odd additions.

Embedded in the pavement and on the base are the old Imperial measurements in feet, yards and chains for local traders to ensure they weren't being diddled.

Also on the base of the column, you can see one of Melly's 43 original drinking fountains (see page 30). On closer inspection, however, the lion's head lacks a certain grandeur and is more Bagpuss than Aslan

Reborn. According to local conservationist/campaigner Patrick Neill, the original drinking spouts were noble affairs. He commissioned local sculptor Tom Murphy to make some more heads from the mould used in restoring the Melly fountain on Woolton Road, and raised £1,000 for their installation. The Council collected them but after three years in which nothing happened, Neill gave up waiting, donated the money to charity and the Council plumped for the B&Q option.

The statue itself has some interesting features: set on a granite pedestal, the Doric column was fashioned from specially quarried stone from Derbyshire to match the colour of St George's Hall and topped off with a cupola upon which stands a bronze statue of the duke, cast from cannons captured from Napoleon.

It's an unusual choice of venue as the duke does not dignify any notable civic buildings with his stare, which is the customary practice when erecting such a statue (e.g. Wyatt's Nelson Memorial on Exchange Flags faces the Queen's Balcony of the Town Hall). The Iron Duke, however, is positioned facing Waterloo to the south-east with a bird's-eye view of the destruction inflicted by developers upon the Futurist Cinema 200 years later.

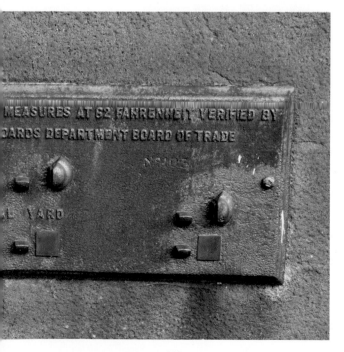

29

MOTHER NOBLETT'S FORMER TOFFEE SHOP

The Toffee Wars

108 London Road, L3 5NL
Just behind Lime Street station

At London Road number 108, the peeling paint above a deli is the last memory of a city-centre branch of Mother Noblett's Toffee Shop (her grave can be found in Anfield cemetery). Take the time to

look up at the fading 'ghost sign' (see page 192): it deserves a special place in football history.

It is tempting to see mascots at football grounds as a recent example of cultural imperialism – an invasion of the beautiful game by the dire 'cheerleader culture' invented by American marketing men in the forlorn hope of transforming the NFL into an international spectator sport.

In the UK every Saturday afternoon, overgrown Muppets trundle along touchlines in the pitiful belief that they are cheering us all up. Sammy The Shrimp at Southend, H'Angus the Monkey (elected mayor of Hartlepool in 2002) and Grantham Town's Isaac the giant Gingerbread Man are all in the running for the UK's worst. And the least said about Wolfie the Wolf's unprovoked attack on Ashton Gate's Three Little Pigs the better. But if, as the song goes, you know your history, it is Everton Football Club that got the ball rolling over a century before clubs engaged marketing departments to take our minds off what is being served up on the pitch.

If you dodge the pubs around Goodison Park and avoid the bars inside the ground, it's still possible to get seated early enough to grab a glimpse of the Toffee Lady circling the pitch and heaving sweets into the crowd. There are many contradictory and improbable versions of how this came about but the following seems to be the most likely.

In the 1700s, when Everton was an attractive village overlooking the port, Molly Bushell made a name for the place by selling Everton Toffee to weekend visitors. Following her death in 1818, the family kept the business going. Competitors sprang up but, when Everton FC got going, Ye Anciente Everton Toffee House (next to the club's Queen's Head HQ) was in prime position to milk the walk-up trade.

When the club moved to Goodison Park, so did the centre of the toffee trade and Mother Noblett's Toffee Shop became the new beneficiary. Unable to use Ma Bushell's patented product, she coated toffees with mint candy and sold them as Everton Mints. In a marketing master stroke, she gained permission from Everton's directors to distribute them into the crowd before kick-off.

The first football club to have a nickname and the world's first mascot

According to legend, Molly Bushell's granddaughter, Jemima, was engaged as the very first Toffee Lady. This probably makes Everton the first club to have a nickname (the Toffees) and Jemima the world's first mascot.

BRIDEWELL STUDIOS

Creative porridge

101 Prescot Street, L7 8UL
0151 263 6730
Open for art classes, occasional exhibitions and on Heritage Open Days
10-min walk from Lime Street station or any bus heading for the Royal
Liverpool University Hospital
Car parking is a nightmare

On the site of what was once 'Rats' Castle' (whose residents threw banquets featuring gourmet dishes of vermin, cats, beetles and spiders) stands one of Liverpool's few surviving 'lock-ups', and the first in the North-West to employ female detectives. This one stopped offering overnight accommodation to local drunks a good few years ago, and, in 1976, the cells and offices of the old Prescot Street Police and Fire Station were converted into artists' studios.

Little was spent on the refurb, so no sleuth is needed to detect its origins. 'Public Enquiries' hatch in the hallway, barred windows, metal doors, an exercise yard and a sign on the stairs for the Detective's Office, this is a strange venue in which to challenge creative boundaries ... but 40 years ago, Liverpool-based artists such as Adrian Henri, Maurice Cockrill and Stephen Broadbent took up residence and did just that. Cockrill's *Nocturne to the City* was painted from the rooftop in 1980 although the view has long gone thanks to a grim development next door.

Sculptor Anish Kapoor was banged up here in 1982, as was singer-songwriter David Gray during a spell busking on Hardman Street and

performing at Peter Kavanagh's: 'I lived in Liverpool for about six years altogether. I wrote a lot of my early songs there. We lived in the old Bridewell prison. I used to live in the little turret. It was the coldest flat I've ever had … so I'd sit there shivering, writing my songs. It was a happy time of my life, something I'll always look back on fondly.'

There is even a fake plaque commemorating Snowy Malone's fatal fall here during the filming of *Boys from the Blackstuff*.

Now a Grade II Listed building owned and run by the artists since 1981, the Bridewell is home to 36 working artisans. Those still doing time here include painters, sculptors, ceramicists, photographers and furniture makers. Resident printmaker Karen Edwards recalls, 'My own granddad was arrested here for being drunk in charge of a bike. When my grandmother found out, she told them to keep him!'

The exercise yard is now a Secret Garden and the building has three ghosts (one happy, one sad and a horse).

Cop shops nearby

Liverpool's Main Bridewell on Cheapside (allegedly connected by tunnels to the law courts in St George's Hall) is now a hotel and the one on Argyle Street is now a pub (see page 20).

The meaning(s) of Scouse: a dish – an identity – a unique accent

According to legend, Lapskaus (good bowlful) was a meat stew brought to Liverpool by Scandinavian sailors and anglicised to 'lobscouse' ... a meat-shy version is known as 'blind Scouse'. Alternatively, Tony Crowley, Professor of English and erstwhile Scouser, suggests that the term was already well established in the English language by the 1700s. It gets an unflattering mention in *The Wooden World Dissected* (1708), Ward's satire of life at sea, and in Smollett's *The Adventures of Peregrine Pickle* (1751), where it is referred to as nothing more than 'a mess of that savoury known by the name of "lob's course"', i.e. a dish fit for a lout. Perhaps the latter-day Vikings plundered the dish from Merseyside. Whichever the true direction, it is not known why it became popular in Liverpool

rather than in other ports such as Hull, Bristol or London.

On post-war 'Scottie Road' (a tough and vibrant community serving the North Docks), meat was still rationed and Tommy Reason (who grew up there) recalls eating 'Scabby-eyed Scouse' – something between the full-blooded carnivore version and the 'blind' variety because 'you'd go "scabby eye'd" looking for the meat'.

Scouse is also a nickname, possibly a term of abuse, but it tends to be the generic name for people from Liverpool, with associations of class: in the past, a distinction was made between 'Liverpolitans' (posh) and 'Liverpudlians' (common), with the term 'Scouse' originally reserved for the 'underclass' of Scotland Road. Nowadays, no self-respecting Evertonian would use 'Liverpudlian' as a form of self-identification, so 'Scouser' is preferable and used by both sets of fans. Scouse, as a reference to Merseyside's distinctive accent or dialect, is a different matter. Its origins in Liverpool's climate and history and possible Irish links are uncertain. According to Prof. Crowley, the term was not used to refer to the local language until the 1950s and has become something of an 'invented tradition', enshrined in popular culture through the efforts of local historians, journalists, entertainers, TV dramatists and documentary film makers: 'Scouse is ... a contemporary example of a mode of cultural representation that is peculiarly British: that curious, powerful and often damaging concatenation of language, class, geography, identity and political significance.'

'Be Scouse, eat Scouse'

Despite lobscouse's reputation as a dish for the poor, the *Literary Gazette* in 1837 tried to promote it as 'a dish fit for the gods' and the poet Wilfred Owen records his father celebrating a new job in Shrewsbury by cooking 'his famous lobscouse'. But you don't need a special reason to tuck in – Maggie May's on Bold Street serves it every day, including Global Scouse Day (GSD).

Started by Liverpool adventurer Graham Hughes (*Guinness Book of Records* as the first person ever to have travelled to every country without flying) and Laura Worthington (of Laura's Little Bakery), GSD is celebrated in pubs and restaurants across Liverpool every 28 February. Participating venues can be found at https://globalscouseday.com

Rob Webb, managing director of Voodou hair salons, has petitioned the queen to have GSD blessed as a national holiday – a kind of Liverpudlian Burns Night.

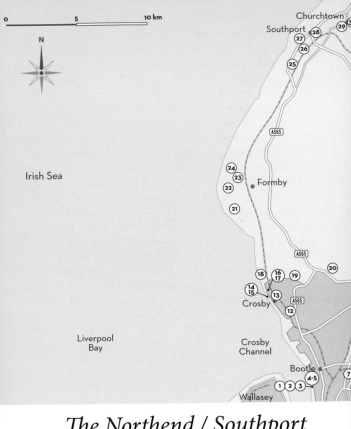

The Northend / Southport

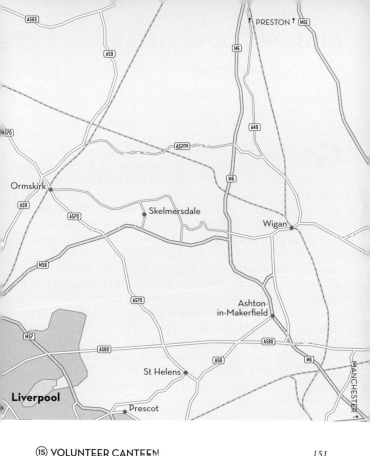

CLARENCE DOCK GATES

'Ireland's second capital'

2 Waterloo Road, L3 7DS (aka 'the Dock Road')
Easiest access by car
Merseyrail to Sandhills, then a 15-min walk, or a 25-min walk from Pier Head

Gazing through the rusting gates which bar entry to the Clarence Dock, it is hard to believe that this is part of a World Heritage Site and regarded as a Jesse Hartley masterpiece. Described in 1841 as 'an extremely handsome specimen of mural masonry', its graving docks 'may be considered amongst the most valuable and handsome of modern appendages to the commercial accommodations of the port'.

Built in 1830 as Liverpool's first steamship dock, it was named in honour of the Duke of Clarence: third in line for the throne, he can be excused for not showing much interest in providing a legitimate heir, as demonstrated by the ten children he sired with the Irish actress Dorothy Jordan. Consequently, he assumed the throne as William IV without legitimate issue. While Victoria waited in the wings for William to pop his regal clogs, Hartley completed the neighbouring dock, named in her honour.

In 1845, Ireland was plunged into the Great Famine, a combination of potato blight, absentee landlords and the greed of their land agents, compounded by a British government dithering between acts of commission and doing nothing at all ('The Almighty, indeed, sent the potato blight, but the English created the famine'). Over five years, the Irish population was decimated by starvation and (for those who could afford the fare) emigration.

As Liverpool offered the closest point of disembarkation for the trip to the New World, the Clarence Dock marks a pivotal moment in the

history of Irish communities at home and abroad. Let down by 'the richest empire on the globe', most of the 1.3 million who 'took the ship' would have trudged their way through these gates to a future in America, Australia, London, Manchester or Birmingham. Many also made a home in the most impoverished parts of Liverpool, creating communities marked for years by religious intolerance and sectarian violence, thankfully a thing of the past.

A plaque marks the momentous role played by Liverpool in the Irish diaspora. (For 30 years, between 1895 and 1925, Scotland Road was the only constituency in England to return an Irish Nationalist MP.)

In 1929, the 'magnificent masonry' of Hartley's dock was filled in and, in keeping with the city's tradition of trashing its heritage, made way for the 'three sisters' (the landmark chimneys of a new power station), itself thankfully demolished in 1998. It has remained derelict ever since and waits to discover what fate Liverpool Waters regeneration scheme has in store for it. According to the masterplan, this might include 'another cluster of tall buildings' and 'some sort of cultural building on the waterfront'.

THE KING'S PIPE

Brown gold

Stanley Dock, L3 0AN (the 'pipe' is on Great Howard Street)
Easiest access by car
Merseyrail to Sandhills, then a 15-min walk, or a 25-min walk from Pier Head

The warehouses, pumping station and bascule bridge over Regent Road are now part of the World Heritage Site listing and well worth a visit. In the south-east corner of the dock, on Great Howard Street, look out for a rare example of a 'King's Pipe'. This can be accessed from Regent Road via Saltney Street (aka 'Pneumonia Alley') and should not be confused with the chimney on Regent Road, which is wrongly identified by the odd webpage as the pipe's location.

The Tobacco Warehouse at the Stanley Dock, built in 1901, gives some idea of the immensity of the trade ... this monster is the largest brick building ever constructed (27 million bricks) and covers 120,000 square metres – at its peak, it could hold around 30,000 tonnes of the stuff and was the largest bonded warehouse in the world. Tobacco would be released for sale on payment of the duty owed and, to ensure that surplus and damaged cargo did not end up as a tax-free perk, the King's Pipe and furnace were installed in the original warehouse in 1855 to incinerate the excess: tax paid or otherwise, tobacco achieves its ultimate purpose and goes up in smoke.

When tobacco was introduced from the New World by sailors in the 17th century, they had no idea of the wealth and misery the pipe-smoking craze would create or the fortunes that would be made on the back of nicotine addiction. James I was one of the earliest opponents of tobacco, which he vilified as 'loathsome to the eye, hatefull to the Nose, harmfull to the braine, dangerous to the lungs ... resembling the horrible Stygian smoke of the pit that is bottomlesse'.

Then, as now, the Government Health Warning was ignored. Miffed by the public rejection of his regal advice, James imposed import duties in 1604: if the populace were intent on smoking themselves to death, they should be made to pay for the pleasure. Despite the deterrents, snuff, chewing tobacco and smoking became popular elements of British culture and were even touted as cures for common ailments such as constipation, scrofula and cancer. In 1665, pipe smoking became a compulsory part of the National Curriculum when schoolboys were instructed to smoke in class as a defence against the Great Plague.

The inevitability of death and taxes is neatly symbolised in one product as tobacco-related deaths currently account for 96,000 a year in the UK and over £12b in revenue to HMRC. It is projected that during the 21st century smoking will kill over 1 billion people worldwide.

STANLEY DOCK BRANCH

A time portal to another world

Stanley Dock, L3 0AN (off Great Howard Street)
canalplan.org.uk/waterway/8u62
Easiest access by car
Merseyrail to Sandhills, then a 15-min walk, or a 25-min walk from Pier Head

Opposite the Tobacco Warehouse and across the four-lane highway which is Great Howard Street, search for a hole in the brick wall lining this side of the road. It looks like war damage, but appearances can be deceptive. This is a time portal to another world: an era of transport that existed prior to the motor car; an industrialised Narnia of railway viaducts, lock gates and towpaths. If it were not for the neat rows of modern terraces each side of the canal, occasional graffiti and the regular clatter of Merseyrail overhead, you would think you were back in the early days of the Industrial Revolution.

The Stanley Dock was originally conceived as the 'world's first integrated dock, canal and railway depot', but the railway and barge docks never got off the drawing board and two warehouses were constructed on the dock instead. Nevertheless, a viaduct for the railway was built in 1848 along with a canal branch completed by Hartley in the same year –

this was designed to give the Leeds and Liverpool Canal (LLC) access to the Stanley Dock and the Mersey beyond. The canal itself stretches for 200 km (the longest in Britain) and passes through 91 locks with a summit of 150 metres excavated entirely by the picks and shovels of navvies. It connected the cotton warehouses of Liverpool to the textile towns of Lancashire and Yorkshire – the original Northern Powerhouse.

Passing beneath the railway viaduct, the dock branch (aka the Stanley Flight) consists of four granite locks which raise the waterway 13.5 metres up from the Liverpool docks to the main canal some 800 metres away. Superseded by the railway and the M62, the canal fell idle and the branch became an industrial wasteland of boatyards, scrap metal dealers and waste disposal units. Over the past 15 years, however, the canals have been renovated and the area restored with new links to the Ribble and the Albert Dock.

The short walk along the branch to the LLC is pleasant enough, but for those who prefer a challenge, here are three possibilities:

• An 8-km walk along the LLC to Litherland (get the train back).

• A 200-km trek to Leeds (Gerry Corden suggests breaking it into 12 separate stages, using a combination of Shanks's pony, public transport and the car: see gerryco23.wordpress.com/walking-the-canal).

• Take on the 3,200-km network of canals stretching from Bristol to Kendal and from London to Ripon: see www.towpathtreks.co.uk.

THE STATUE OF DOMINION PUB ④

'He puts on women's clothing and hangs around in bars'

Bankfield Enterprise Hub, 32 Bankfield Street, L20 8EJ
Merseyrail to Bank Hall station
By car, take the A565 out of town and turn left down Bankfield Street

At the junction of Bankfield Street and Regent Road stands the derelict Dominion pub crowned by the statue of a 19th-century frontiersman. Axe in hand and loyal mutt at his feet, he gazes out across Canada Dock. This was the hub of Liverpool's trade with North America.

The link dates back to the 1770s, when merchants were attracted to the plentiful supply of timber. By 1852, some 963,000 cubic metres of Canadian planks were coming into Liverpool, along with 283,000 cubic metres of pine, in around 373 ships. (Liverpool in Nova Scotia shares a history of shipbuilding as well as the name.) In 1859, Jesse Hartley's Canada Dock opened to cope with the trade in wood, fish products and wheat. Liverpool was also heavily involved in Canadian emigration until 1971, with the Dominion Line a prominent player in the export of human cargo.

As the pub carries the name of the shipping line and the character on the roof is gripping an axe, it is fair to assume that this is in celebration of the timber trade, but not everyone agrees. Ruth Gregory (on www. picturesofengland.com) suggests it may show the mythical American giant Paul Bunyan, who has at least eight roadside statues to his name across the northern forests of Minnesota, Wisconsin and Michigan. On the other hand, Jimmy Conelly, who works at Terry's Timber Yard and used to drink in the pub, assures the character is a cotton picker ...

Unfortunately, the pub was closed by the authorities, so we may never know the true story. According to the *Echo*, the already derelict pub was raided by police in 2008 on suspicion of operating as a brothel. They found four working girls and a client along with PVC costumes, sex toys and a list of regulars. Based on this evidence, and in a spirit of even-handedness, they promptly arrested the girls and let the man go. It now houses refurbished commercial units topped off with this iconic logo.

NEARBY
Loco RH 224347 ⑤

At the top of Bankfield Street you will find a loco engine. You might assume (wrongly) that it was one of the many Mersey Docks & Harbour Board shunters that shifted cargo to depots around the town (preceded by a flag-waving guard). Sadly, the only relic of the MDHB fleet is in storage, due to lack of museum space. According to railway historian Dave Marden, it's an RH 224347, which never actually worked the docks but was installed in 1998 in recognition of the work of the Merseyside Development Corporation and the redevelopment of the A565 as 'Atlantic Avenue'.

REMEMBRANCE GARDEN OF ST LUKE THE EVANGELIST

*The only church in the world that's within
a football stadium*

16 Goodison Rd, L4 4EL
www.stlukeswalton.org
*Matchdays: 2 hours before KO. Sun 12 noon–12.45 pm, following church
service (11am–12 noon)*
See directions on the Everton website:
www.evertonfc.com/content/club/directions

The pitch at HNK Trogir's football stadium is sandwiched between two UNESCO World Heritage Sites. Fulham's ground has a cottage incorporated into the Johnny Haynes Stand. But only Goodison Park has its very own church. Built between 1899 and 1901, St Luke

the Evangelist sits between the Main Stand and the Gwladys Street end.

To the first-time visitor, the red brick church jutting out from the edge of a (Royal Blue) football stadium may seem incongruous, but to Evertonians it is part of their history. Many of the faithful will have visited the parish hall next door for a cuppa and a pre-match prayer or to browse the match-day stalls in search of a rare programme from yesteryear. Some may have attended services at the church, but few will have set foot in St Luke's Garden of Remembrance. A tiny strip of land hemmed in by a stadium forced to grow around it, the garden is the final resting place for the ashes of fans who refuse to say goodbye. It is open on match days for those wishing to pay their respects, but most fans scurry past oblivious to its quiet charm.

A symbol of the link between football and the 'purity movement'

In the second half of the 19th century, Victorian Britain was gripped by a moral panic in which concerns about economic and social decline, military power and Empire became confused with anxieties over 'racial hygiene', masculinity and sexual deviance. According to writer David Winner, the issue was first confronted by public school headmasters: inspired by 'Muscular Christianity', they employed 'organised sport and sexual repression' as the antidote to moral decline, effeminacy and 'beastliness' (masturbation was condemned as the cause of lunacy and early death). 'Athleticism ... was a motor for the muscular new imperialism, for militarism and conformism. Suppression of sexuality, individuality – and even thought itself – were essentially elements of this process and were encoded in the games themselves.'

Within a year of arriving at nearby St Domingo Chapel in 1877, the Rev. Ben Swift Chambers had got local lads playing football and Everton F.C. was born. Little did he know that he was founding two clubs or the bitter rivalry this would unleash (see page 140).

Why Everton can't play early Sunday games

As part of a long-standing agreement with the church, Everton do not play early Sunday games, a rule that has survived Rupert Murdoch's conquest of the fixture list.

The Bullens Road Stand at Goodison Park was built by Archibald Leitch, who also designed Fulham's Johnny Haynes Stand and its cottage.

ANFIELD CATACOMBS

A hidden Jem

Anfield cemetery, Priory Road, L4 2SL
friendsofanfield.com
Weekdays 9am–4.45pm, Sun 9am–12 noon
By bus to Stanley Park: see either www.evertonfc.com/content/club/directions
or www.liverpoolfc.com/fans/fan-experience/getting-to-anfield

Opened in 1863, Anfield cemetery is one of the largest in Europe and home to the fourth-oldest crematorium in the country. The sectarian squabbles that marked the lives of the inhabitants are repeated in death as the graveyard is segregated according to religious affiliation (C of E, Catholic and General). Over time, the carved stone catacombs (also segregated by belief) fell into a ruinous state following the predations of grave robbers and general vandalism and had to be fenced off. Thanks to the efforts of the Friends of Anfield Cemetery, and with financial support from Liverpool City Council and Historic England, they are now being restored to their former glory.

In the company of John Halliday, the leading authority on the cemetery and its 98,000 graves, we are taken on an unofficial tour of the headstones and the stories they have to tell. We meet wealthy merchants, people with links to the *Victory*, the *Titanic*, the Charge of the Light Brigade, the American Civil War, both Everton and Liverpool football clubs and even see the burial site of a car that had been part of an insurance scam.

You can book on a tour organised by the Friends or just turn up for a wander; you'll probably bump into John anyway – he tells me he walks here every day and has not had a holiday in 41 years! As the plot records were removed from the lodge, he is a walking record of who sleeps where and is often called upon to identify graves for relatives seeking the final resting place of an ancestor (he can be contacted on 0151 263 5982).

Notable graves

James Maybrick: 'murder' victim and self-proclaimed 'Jack the Ripper' (see page 204).

Alexander MacLennan: Isambard Kingdom Brunel's chief engineer. Saved the SS *Great Eastern* during a storm in 1859.

Michael Holliday (aka 'the British Bing Crosby'): Liverpool seaman turned crooner. Popular during the 1950s with two No. 1 singles, he suffered from stage fright and depression, committing suicide in 1963 (his headstone bears his real name, Norman Milne).

Jem Mace ('the father of modern boxing'): Bare-Knuckle Champion of England, he became the first World Champion in 1870 when he defeated Tom Allen in St Louis. He was still boxing at 60 and ran a boxing club in Liverpool. On his death, he ended up in an unmarked grave but was reinterred here in 2002.

STANLEY HOUSE

The home of King John

73 Anfield Road, L4 0TF
See directions on the Liverpool F.C. website:
www.liverpoolfc.com/fans/fan-experience/getting-to-anfield

Standing in the shadow of Anfield Stadium and ignored by most
fans is Stanley House, where Liverpool F.C. was founded in 1892.
The club's origins, however, go back to 1877, when the Rev. Ben Swift
Chambers arrived at the St Domingo Chapel and founded a cricket
team ... but in the winter months it was football that drew lads from far
across the district. At a meeting in the Queen's Head Hotel in 1878, St
Domingo became Everton F.C.

For a time Everton played at Anfield Road, but the club president, John Houlding, was also the landlord of the Anfield ground and owner of the Sandon pub next door. When he insisted on a rent rise for the pitch, an acrimonious split developed which tapped into more deep-seated divisions. The original driving force behind football in the area had come from the Methodists, motivated by the principles of 'Muscular Christianity' and abstinence. Houlding, however, was a Tory councillor and Orangeman with extensive brewery interests who insisted that only his beer could be served within the ground.

Following a bitter dispute (no pun intended), Houlding gave the Everton committee notice to quit Anfield and the Blues moved across Stanley Park, taking their ball with them. Houlding was sacked from the board and (hard to believe today) attempted to hold on to the Everton name. The FA sided with the original club and Houlding called a meeting of like-minded ex-Evertonians at his home in Stanley House on 15 March 1892, when the decision was taken to name the new club after the city.

Despite initial opposition from the hometown rugby club, which already had the name, Houlding's breakaway team eventually took to the old Everton ground with a new name and wearing the blue and white kit Everton had left behind. Oddly enough, Everton played in red shirts until 1895, when they reverted to blue. The following year, when Liverpool could afford a strip of their own, they turned out in red and white – the dye was cast!

Stanley House still stands on Anfield Road next to the ground, but a neglected grave discovered in Shepley Methodist Chapel near Huddersfield is the place to pay homage. Restored by both clubs with a new headstone, the epitaph reads: 'Ben Swift Chambers, who set the ball rolling that led to the birth of Everton and Liverpool football clubs.'

DEANE ROAD HEBREW CEMETERY

The city's oldest surviving Jewish burial ground

Deane Road, Kensington, L7 0ET
www.facebook.com/deaneroadcemetery
Third Sunday of every month 12 noon–4pm
Bus 8, 9, or 10 from Queen Square. Alight at Capaldi's

Opposite Capaldi's Cafe, Deane Road leads us to an impressive screen wall rendered in stucco and stone in the Greek Revival style. Its Doric entrance is flanked by fluted columns and has an architrave bearing an inscription from the Book of Job ('Here the weary are at rest'). This is the entrance to a Jewish cemetery that spent half its life sealed off from the world.

The Jewish community in Liverpool dates back to the 1740s and its Broadgreen cemetery has a section containing remains interred here when the earlier cemeteries were closed. Deane Road, however, is the city's oldest surviving Jewish burial ground. It was designed in 1836 by Samuel Rowland (best known for the church of St Bride's on Percy Street). It closed for burials in 1929 and quickly fell into disrepair, the weary's rest disturbed by vandals, fly tippers and the encroachment of nature. It was Grade II Listed in 1975, but until a coordinated restoration effort in 2007, the cemetery looked doomed.

A Lottery award, private donations and volunteer labour transformed the place: the entrance, boundary walls and gates were restored, headstones repaired, wild flowers planted and a Heritage Centre added. It has become a fitting tribute to the men and women who established Liverpool's Jewish community during the 19th century and had been all but forgotten.

Wealthy merchants, politicians, philanthropists, artisans, bankers and bankrupts are commemorated here and the map from the Heritage Centre does a useful job in identifying where to find them. Here is a small list:

David Lewis: probably the best-known resident; founder of a nationwide chain of department stores (including Selfridges) and the iconic Lewis's Department Store in Ranelagh Street. A great benefactor, who left his entire fortune to charity.

Charles Mozley: the only Jewish person to hold the title of mayor.

Humphrey Hime: acclaimed violinist and music publisher; his grandson built Hime's Music Hall (52 Bold Street).

John Raphael Isaac: artist; well known for his lithograph of Liverpool taken from a balloon in 1859.

David Jacob Isaacson: grave marked by a severed granite column that represents 'a life cut short'.

In 2011, the first service in 80 years commemorated the life of Lyon Samson, a pauper buried without a headstone. The memorial tablet was erected by his descendants 168 years after his death.

BLUEBELL WOOD

'Sliding unseen beneath the trees'

Higher Lane, L9 9DJ
Merseyrail to Fazakerley station, then walk back along Longmoor Lane towards town
By car, take A505 from town and turn right down Higher Lane (adjacent to Emmanuel Church)

Sandwiched between Fazakerley Hospital and Altcourse Prison is a woodland that the inmates of both institutions would relish given half a chance. Approaching by road, it's hard to imagine that this haven exists, tucked away behind the busy thoroughfare of North Liverpool. But drop off the main drag into Higher Lane and the cul-de-sac ends in a glorious wood – best visited in late spring to catch the blue carpet spread beneath a canopy of ancient woodland, some of it at least 1,000 years old. An entrance on the left over the River Alt leads into the wood, following well-worn tracks.

The wood is a remnant of the Norman estate granted to the de Fazakerley family in the 12th century – this brought them into conflict with the de Waltons next door. In the 14th century, Robert de Fazakerley (a ruthless bastard with an eye for the occasional land grab) brought the simmering rivalry to a head when his militia booted John de Walton out of the manor. On pain of a fine, the manor was returned and the dispute was finally settled when Robert married Ellen de Walton.

During the Civil War, the Fazakerleys sided with the Royalists and had their lands confiscated for treason. According to legend, Nicholas de Fazakerley squirrelled away the family fortune in leather pouches around the area for safekeeping but was killed at Liverpool in 1643, leaving no map ... so keep your eyes peeled!

Speaking of squirrels, the woods are believed to be the last habitat of coexisting red and grey colonies in the UK. The horse chestnuts date from the Norman Conquest, giving us the name of our oldest game, 'Conkers'. There is also evidence of later cultivation when Jaques Myers built Harbreck House in 1850 and had an avenue of trees planted up to its entrance (see if you can spot the odd monkey puzzle tree among the natural woodland). In the 1950s, the mansion was added to the spiralling list of Liverpool historic buildings to get the wrecking ball; only debris remains.

AINTREE GRAND PRIX CIRCUIT ⑪

The world's first track-based motor club

Melling Road, Aintree, L10 8LF
For events, see www.aintree.org.uk and www.liverpoolmotorclub.com
Train to Aintree station, then 15-min walk

Everyone has heard of the Grand National but, unless you live within earshot of Aintree Racecourse, you probably don't know that it has its very own racing circuit. Opened in 1954, it is still the only purpose-built Grand Prix circuit in the country and retains the original layout, which weaves its way in and out of the steeplechase course.

Aintree staged its first British Grand Prix in 1955 – it was won by the legendary Stirling Moss in a Mercedes-Benz (the first time a British driver had done so on home soil). Two years later, he returned to lift the Grand Prix d'Europe, this time in a British car (another first). Aintree staged a total of 12 Formula One races, with Jim Clark winning the last Grand Prix held here in 1962. Subsequently the British Grand Prix was shared between Silverstone and Brands Hatch.

The Aintree Circuit Club, however, remains the world's first track-based motor club, with a sixty-year history. It continues to host regular events and specials for bike and car enthusiasts. Members get free entry to all events and, if you fancy yourself as a budding Lewis Hamilton, membership entitles you to apply for a Motor Sport Association National Competition Licence – vital for entry into more 'serious' events around the country.

The Liverpool Motor Club also holds events at the circuit for enthusiasts who want to enter their own car on Track Days (for a driving experience unhampered by speed cameras and traffic lights) or the more competitive Aintree Sprints (entrants must pre-book on their website). As a descendant of the Liverpool Self-Propelled Traffic Association (which ran hill climbs on Everton Brow in the 1890s), the LMC is the oldest motor club in the UK.

All ACC and LMC events are open to the public, who can pay on the day.

A steeplechase was originally a cross-country horse race from one village church steeple to another – hence its name. Founded in 1836, the Grand National is the world's most famous steeplechase.

POTTER'S BARN

Napoleon's nemesis

Cambridge Road, L21 1EW
Merseyrail to Waterloo station, or bus 53 or 47 from Queen Square
15 min from city centre by car. Take the A565 until the junction with
Cambridge Road, then take a left

The town of Waterloo takes its name from the famous battle (see box opposite). A permanent reminder of the town's association can be found at Potter's Barn, a Grade II Listed gatehouse and stables originally designed as part of the Tudor-arched gateway to a private estate. The owner never completed the project, but the outbuildings, designed to replicate a farmhouse (La Haye Sainte) crucial to the battle, survive to this day as an entrance to the public park.

La Haye Sainte in Belgium was (and still is) a walled farmhouse at the foot of an escarpment around which the troops of Napoleon and Wellington grappled for advantage. Realising its strategic importance, Wellington posted a group of 400 Hanoverian refugees garrisoned at Bexhill-on-Sea (the King's German Legion) to defend the position. Hopelessly outnumbered by six to one, they maintained an 'epic defence' until they ran out of ammunition ... by which time Blücher's cavalry had arrived to steal all the plaudits.

For the first time in British military history, a campaign medal was awarded to every soldier who took part. In 2015, a commemorative copy

was struck to honour the 200th anniversary of the victory and distributed by the Royal Mint while stocks lasted (the bronze one is free but a solid gold version, with ribbon, will set you back £345). The Great British public are clearly not as patriotic as they used to be because 200waterloo. co.uk still have a few of the 'limited edition' freebies on their hands. All you need is £2.50 for postage and the medal can be yours.

Potters Barn, showing entrance, Seaforth.

Prior to the Battle of Waterloo in 1815, Crosby Seabank was home to a handful of fisherfolk and the odd farmer, but was beginning to attract the attention of wealthy Liverpolitans keen to escape the town and attracted to the novel pursuit of sea-bathing. Day trips were encouraged by a regular stage coach service and the building of a hotel, completed on the first anniversary of the battle.

Keen to be associated with a winning brand, the owners changed the name at the last minute from the prosaic Crosby Seabank Hotel to the Waterloo Hotel and, as the railway arrived, a small town grew up: it attracted sea captains and merchants, and the streets were named in honour of those associated with the battle. Feeling they had played their part in launching the town, the hotel owners then abbreviated the name to The Royal, but a black tie Waterloo Dinner still celebrates the association. The main course being ... Beef Wellington.

THE PAINTING
OF THE LIVERPOOL PIGEON

'There's every race and colour of face, there's every kind of name
But the pigeons on the Pier Head, they treat you all the same'

14 Endbutt Lane, L23 0TR
0151 949 0341
liverpoolpigeon.wordpress.com
10-min walk from Blundellsands and Crosby stations, or bus 53 from Queen Square

- 148 -

Above the entrance to one of Liverpool's most recent microbreweries and on the wall of the pub inside is a replica of a painting by Josef Smit celebrating the existence of a bird named after the city. The Liverpool Pigeon only serves real ale and ciders and has twice been voted Pub of the Year by the local branch of CAMRA. They recently teamed up with the reborn Satterthwaites Bakehouse, so you can enjoy 'the best pork pies in the known universe' along with a decent pint.

According to pest control expert Ken Lewis, there are probably over 1 million pigeons in Liverpool ... overhead, under your feet, feasting on McRubbish. They're everywhere and it costs over £160,000 a year to clean up after them. So, you might ask, what's so special about a Scouse pigeon? But then you've never met *Caloenus maculata*, which is without doubt the most secretive bird you're ever likely to come across. This is largely due to its being extinct for over 230 years but also because the only surviving specimen is kept under lock and key in Liverpool's World Museum. In 1783, it was part of a pair documented by English ornithologist John Latham, who described it as the spotted green pigeon and claimed it as a new species in his *General History of Birds*.

One of the birds was sold to the 13th Earl of Derby in the 1800s from the collection of General Thomas Davies for £2.1 and ended up in Knowsley Hall. In 1851, it was part of the bequest which formed the original collection of the National Museum of Liverpool. As its sibling disappeared, the unique status of the 'Liverpool pigeon' was assured. Ignored for 150 years, it was officially recognised in 2008 by Bird Life International as an 'extinct full species'. In 2014, as a result of a ground-breaking genetic study of DNA extracted from a couple of feathers, the Liverpool pigeon was declared 'a distant relation to the Nicobar pigeon, the Rodrigues solitaire and the dodo of Mauritius', all descendants of 'island-hopping' ancestors.

Due to its fragile condition, the relic is protected from daylight in a controlled storage environment and continues its elusive existence out of the public gaze. However, the Latham painting can be seen in his *Synopsis of Birds* and the one by Smit is in the Bulletin of the Liverpool Museums. Anyone with a genuine ornithological interest in seeing this unique specimen must apply to the Vertebrate Zoology Department at the World Museum for an authorised visit.

BEACH LAWN HOUSE

'Titanic town'

13 Beach Lawn, Crosby, L22 8QA
Merseyrail to Waterloo station or bus 53 from Queen Square
Easily reached by car on the A565

Built by Thomas 'Baccy' Ismay, the Grade II Listed villa at the end of Beach Lawn appears to have had its unlucky number removed from the gateposts. A quick dip into the family history may explain why. After escaping from Maryport, in Cumbria, the young Thomas became apprenticed to shipbrokers in Liverpool at the age of 16. Following a time at sea, he entered into a partnership with an old sea dog, but they quarrelled over the future of the industry: good old-fashioned wood or common-sense-defying iron? Thomas backed the winner and went on to take over the ailing White Star Line at the age of 30.

He must having been doing well because he had this new family house built on the fashionable Crosby Seabank in the 1860s. It was here that his ill-fated and infamous son, Joseph, grew up ... later to be vilified after the disaster as the owner of the *Titanic* who secured himself a berth in a lifeboat.

Bad luck seems to have run in the family as the *Titanic* was not the only disaster to occur on their watch. In 1873, the RMS *Atlantic* went down off the coast of Nova Scotia with the loss of 535 lives – all the women and children perished. One of the crew who died was later revealed as a woman in disguise. A shipmate recalled at the time: 'I didn't know Bill was a woman. He used to take his grog as regular as any of

us, and was always begging or stealing tobacco. He was a good fellow, though, and I'm sorry he was a woman.'

By an odd coincidence, the captain of the *Titanic* (unlike his boss, he went down with the ship) lived just along the seafront at 17 Marine Terrace, a small stuccoed and slate-roofed villa that forms part of a pretty pastel-shaded terrace. For £5 the present owner will sell you a copy of her book detailing the main features of the house.

A memorial in St Faith's Church in Great Crosby commemorates the ship's chief engineer, who also came from Maryport.

NEARBY
Volunteer Canteen

Behind Marine Crescent is a Victorian pub with the strangest moniker. The Volunteer Canteen derives its name from the 1840s Methodist chapel next door, which became the drill hall for Boer War volunteers who adopted the pub as their canteen. It then became the Bijou Theatre and, later, the Bijou Electric Picture House. It was demolished in the 1980s but the pub survives. Despite a CAMRA suggestion that the pub still has old-fashioned bell push barmaid service, the bells were removed a few years ago. 'Thank God for that,' says Jen from behind the hatch. 'They used to drive you mad.'

ST NICHOLAS FOUNTAIN

All that remains of a house with a sinister pagan link

At junction of The Serpentine North and Burbo Bank Road North, Crosby L23 6UT

Merseyrail to Blundellsands & Crosby or Hall Road, or bus 53 from Queen Square to Crosby, then 206 circular from Crosby (Merchant Taylors) to the Serpentine

In Blundellsands, a grand sweep of coastal road (the Serpentine) was home to several wealthy 19th-century merchants. At a fork in the road, a Gothic sandstone drinking fountain is all that remains of a house with a sinister pagan link. Unfortunately, modern developments with rows of Lego shoe boxes have replaced the grand old mansions ... including the one-time home of the Gardner family and birthplace of Gerald Brousseau Gardner who, spookily, entered this world on Friday 13 June 1884. He is widely regarded as the father of modern witchcraft, the only religion that England has ever given the world.

One version has his birthplace as The Glen, although Heselton's biography claims that the family moved to nearby Ingle Lodge before Gerald's birth. According to local researcher, Al Clinton, Ingle Green now marks the spot of the Lodge, while all that remains of The Glen is St Nicholas fountain, which was erected outside the family home to deter 'cockle mollies' from asking at the house for water.

Gardner came from a long line of wealthy, powerful people, including two witches: a Scottish ancestor, Grissell, burned at the stake in 1610; and his paternal granny. His own father was prone to strip bollock-naked in public at the first hint of rain while Gerald himself was a fervent nudist. During a life abroad, which included a spell as Governor Inspector of Opium Dens in Malaya, he became fascinated with the occult.

On his retirement, Gardner was initiated into a New Forest coven under the auspices of local witch 'Old Dorothy' Clutterbuck. He then set about the revival of witchcraft despite the fact that it was a crime under the Witchcraft Act of 1735. He attracted many followers (at home and abroad), became 'resident witch' at the Museum of Magic and Witchcraft on the Isle of Man and visited Aleister Crowley ('the Wickedest Man in the World') on his deathbed. His greatest self-proclaimed achievement was to thwart Hitler's plans for invasion by summoning a magical 'cone of power' somewhere in the New Forest.

NEARBY

Park Drive Key Park ⑰

Buried off the grand sweep of the Serpentine is one of the few surviving members-only Key Parks in the country, with a waiting list of three years. If you can't wait that long, catch a glimpse from the pedestrian access on Park Drive.

FORT CROSBY

A Top Secret secret

HM Coastguard Station, Waterloo, L23 8SY
www.academia.edu/17314554/
Forgotten_Fort_Crosby_Dune_Heritage_Revealed
Merseyrail to Hall Road
30-min drive to Crosby Coastguard Station (Pay & Display car park), then
short walk through sand dunes (beware of rabbit holes)

Hidden among the sand dunes beyond the car park at the Coastguard Station are the crumbling remnants of a remarkable chapter in the history of aerial warfare. Largely forgotten and hard to find, these are the remains of Fort Crosby.

For years, the entrance to the Mersey was regarded as a potential weak spot for enemy invasion from the sea, but no serious attempt was made to guard the port until the threat of seaborne invasion had all but gone. Following official warnings that Liverpool was 'totally unprotected by any defences', gun batteries were eventually constructed at Fort Crosby and Fort Perch Rock on the opposite bank in 1906.

Merseyside escaped being a direct target during the First World War but, by the outbreak of the Second, the threat was not so much from the sea as the air and Fort Crosby formed part of the air-raid reporting system operated by the Royal Observer Corps. Searchlights and an anti-aircraft battery were added, but the most intriguing aspect of the place is its use of decoys to trick German bomb crews into hitting the wrong target – the Formby decoy was one of 14 'Starfish' decoys used to deflect attention away from Liverpool.

Geoff Edmonds, who was stationed there, recalls: 'The Starfish site was a layout of docks and other buildings, a lighting system and explosive detonations to fool the Luftwaffe into thinking there was something down there worth bombing. Attracting bombs to fall onto the shore, sea or open country, thus saving dock and city areas.'

It has been estimated that there were 237 Starfish sites across the country, protecting centres crucial to the war effort, and that they succeeded in diverting 730 air raids and saving as many as 2,500 lives.

In 2015, archaeologist Alison Burns' investigation of the Crosby site revealed that the control room for the Starfish is still there, as are gun placements and the odd anti-aircraft shelter.

Between 1945 and 1950, the camp buildings were converted into a POW camp and the surrounding beaches became a dumping ground for wartime rubble.

The beach of bricks

At first glance, the beach (from Fort Crosby to Hightown) looks like the creation of white-van builders keen to avoid dumping charges at the local tip. However, closer inspection reveals that it is a dump site of some significance. Rather than a transgression of local authority waste disposal regulations, it was deliberately planted here as a matter of post-war policy.

Despite the old joke that the city's planners have done more to destroy Liverpool's architectural heritage than Hitler, the Blitz was the most devastating attack on any UK city outside London during the Second World War. It was intended to be. Liverpool was the key port for merchant shipping, handling 90% of imported war materials; it was a naval repair base, home to several munitions factories and HQ of the Western Approaches Command. Given its strategic importance, it is not surprising that Liverpool was top of the Luftwaffe's target list. In 1941, Admiral Raeder sent a memo to Hitler suggesting that 'an early concentrated attack on Britain was necessary, on Liverpool for example, so that the whole nation will feel the effects'.

The first air raid took place in August 1940, but the first week in May 1941 was the most punishing; German planes dropped 870 tonnes of high-explosive bombs and over 112,000 incendiary bombs, starting fires throughout Merseyside.

When the blitzkrieg over Merseyside came to an end after an unrelenting 18-month campaign, almost 4,000 civilians had perished, over 7,000 had been injured and thousands made

homeless. Much of the cityscape had been transformed for ever – the Customs House was demolished following a direct hit and the 'Bombed-Out Church' on Berry Street still stands as a reminder of a war that introduced the world to the horrors of 'strategic bombing'.

Historic landmarks, public buildings, popular shops, pubs and restaurants were gone for ever, but what to do with the mountains of rubble left behind? The answer was to shift it by the lorry load to the Sefton coast, where it was banked up along the beach to act as a defence against the encroaching waves. As Tom Fairclough tells us in his evocative blog (http://collateral.foliohd.com), '(The rubble) remains there, with the sea washing clean, re-shaping and smoothing it every day for nearly 70 years, slowly returning to nature. It is still recognisable as parts of the public buildings, workplaces and homes destroyed by the bombs and fires of 1940 and 1941.'

Beachcombing amongst the detritus of war, it is possible to stumble across vestiges of Liverpool's lost heritage – Victorian bricks, stone lintels and countless pieces of peacetime bric-a-brac.

HARKIRK CHAPEL

19

'Once a Catholic ...'

Crosby Hall, Little Crosby, L23 4UA
Restricted access: see website for information on summer tours and the annual Mass
www.stmaryslittlecrosby.org.uk
Merseyrail to Hall Road, then a 25-min walk, or bus 53 from Queen Square to
Crosby (Islington), then 206 circular to Little Crosby
By car, take A565 to Great Crosby and left at the roundabout. B5193 to Little
Crosby. Lion Gates mark the entrance to Crosby Hall

Inside the walled estate of Crosby Hall, at the end of a woodland trail, is a memorial chapel dedicated to local recusants buried here in defiance of the Established Church following the Reformation. In a deeply Catholic community such as Little Crosby (claimed to this day as 'the oldest extant Roman Catholic village in England'), resistance was a duty that came at a price: the Harkirk (a Norse word meaning 'grey church') is a 19th-century shrine that commemorates their struggle 300 years earlier. As such, it marks the site of a very rare recusant burial ground, an important symbol of Catholic persecution and resistance.

Henry VIII lived and died a Catholic. He was a staunch defender of the faith apart from those irritating bits about the authority of the Pope and the sanctity of marriage. The confusion over his attitude to the Reformation was not helped by Henry's habit of burning both Catholics and Protestants for heresy. This exemplary zeal inspired his daughters, who took it in turns to persecute both.

Under the reign of Elizabeth, this was bad news for the Blundell family and their tenants: Catholic recusants could be executed for heresy

or treason (priests were guilty of both by virtue of their ordination), fined for non-attendance at Sunday Service and refused burial in consecrated ground. (In secret funerals, 'som were layd in the fields, som in Gardens, and others in Highwayes'.) In 1590, the Blundells escaped the death penalty for harbouring priests but were imprisoned in Lancaster Castle.

In 1610, the vicar of St Helen's Church at Sefton refused burial to a local Catholic woman – she was interred in a shallow grave on common land, where she was sniffed out by foraging pigs 'and had her Corps pulld out by hoggs and used accordingly'. Horrified, William Blundell donated a plot of land on the site of an Anglo-Saxon Harkirk for the burial of local Catholics. On the main track from the village to the church at Sefton, it stood as a very visible reminder of the local recusancy: 'more secret now than it was then,' reckons present incumbent, Mark Blundell.

During the first recusant burial, a hoard of silver coins dating back to Alfred the Great was discovered and melted down to create a chalice (since disappeared) and a pyx (now in the British Museum). During the 1620s, the fines for bunking off Divine Service were reimposed by James I, sparking two bloody altercations with the Sheriff's men (Little Crosby 2 – Sheriff 0). In the 1626 replay, the Sheriff fielded his first team – bigger, fitter, well-trained and armed. The villagers were routed and, in a spiteful act of revenge, the burial ground was trashed.

All but forgotten, the site was restored in 1889 by Colonel Nicholas Blundell, who raised a memorial chapel to commemorate the 131 recusants buried here. Their names are recorded on a tablet in the chapel and relics of the three headstones to survive the Sheriff's vandalism are incorporated in the brickwork by the entrance.

20

LUNT MEADOWS NATURE RESERVE

One of the UK's foremost Mesolithic sites

Lunt Village, L29 7WL
www.liverpoolmuseums.org.uk/mol/archaeology/projects/lunt-meadows/index.aspx
www.lancswt.org.uk/nature-reserves/lunt-meadows
Bus 133 (Cumfybus, hourly service from Waterloo interchange, Crosby). Alight at Lunt Village
By car, take A565 and turn right up Long Lane, then right again at Lunt Road

Lunt Meadows is a recently restored wetland nature reserve on the River Alt, where 77 hectares was excavated in 2012 to provide a flood storage basin. Now a mixed habitat of open water, reed bed and marshland, it is an ideal home for waterfowl, waders, water voles and dragonflies. Deep in this desolate sanctuary to lapwing, redshank, warblers and the Marsh Harrier, it is difficult to believe that you're only some 15km away from the Liver Birds.

Inadvertently, the scheme has returned the wetlands to their prehistoric state and, in the process, uncovered a settlement no one has clapped eyes on for 7,000 years. It turns out to be one of the foremost Mesolithic sites in the UK. Protected by floodwater for millennia, the site has been undisturbed by ploughing and drainage, and has consequently been preserved as a unique settlement of hunter-gatherers.

According to Ron Cowell, curator of prehistoric archaeology at the Museum of Liverpool, the swathe of wetland sandwiched between the sea and an extensive forest would have been an ideal habitat for Mesolithic hunter-gatherers. As it gives up its secrets, the site reveals a semi-permanent, possibly seasonal, dwelling place of several huts which may have existed over a lengthy period and been revisited regularly by succeeding generations of family-based bands of hunters.

Artefacts include flint tools, weaponry and a stone 'altar' that may indicate some ceremonial significance for the place. These treasures are preserved at the Atkinson Museum in Southport. Such finds challenge the conventional paradigm which portrays such people as rootless predators. As Ron Cowell puts it, 'The big thing is the integration of landscape and settlement and people.' It appears that flooding of the plain made it unfit for human habitation and the residents eventually abandoned the site to the encroaching tides. It is possible that they became the ancestors of the Formby Beach footprint makers 10 km away (see page 168).

Ron is now approaching retirement but shows no sign of putting his feet up. 'This must be the biggest and most important site ever dug by one person,' he quipped and, as we left, he returned to the task armed with a trowel and a goody bag. He may have been joking, but it looked very much like a one-man band to me.

LOST RESORT TRAIL
OF FORMBY-BY-THE-SEA

Tiptoe through the sand dunes

Lifeboat Road, Formby, L37 2EB
www.formbycivicsociety.org.uk/ravenmeols_walks_leaflet_2015_red.pdf
Merseyrail to Formby station or by car via A565 and B5424

From the car park on Lifeboat Road, signposts for the Lost Resort Trail guide you through the sand dunes to Raven Meols, where a scheme to rival Southport as a seaside resort was launched in 1876. The promenade, hotel and houses have been largely reclaimed by the ever-shifting dunes. However, a hollow to the right of the trail contains the old Second World War rifle range, daubed with uninspiring urban graffiti.

All that remains of Formby-by-the-Sea are Seabank House at the beach end of Albert Road and, at its inland junction with Alexandra Road, Beach Lawn and Sandhills Cottage opposite. Off Albert Road, look out for rare black poplars which mark the remains of 'The Briars'.

Follow the marked trail opposite Seabank House to the Devil's Hole. Local researcher, Reg Yorke, regards this huge crater as 'our best blowout' ... probably caused by German bombers tricked into overshooting their target by the nearby 'Starfish' decoy (see page 154). However, the trail skirts it without ever indicating a left fork into the crater, so it's easy to end up on the MOD rifle range. At this point, it's probably a good idea to take the 2-km detour imposed by this lethal obstacle and follow the perimeter fence all the way around it. The chief military objective of the place seems to be the destruction of any hope of a Sunday lie-in for the good people of Hightown, gratified no doubt to hear their taxes being so well spent.

Continue through the village to discover the remains of a submerged prehistoric forest on the foreshore beneath Blundellsands Sailing Club.

On the beach, the ruins of the Formby Lifeboat Station can still be found. This was built in the 1770s by Liverpool Dock Master and reformed pirate William Hutchinson as a 'boat and station for saving lives'. It was the first in the world, the Corporation paying crews 'a guinea, or more ... for every human life that is saved'.

The lifeboat was powered by oarsmen and drawn to the sea by horses, but the station was so far from the tide that it was almost useless. According to Green Sefton's project officer, John Dempsey, 'If you got into trouble in Liverpool Bay and relied on the Formby lifeboat ... you were in big trouble'. It was quickly succeeded by alternative stations but survived as a cafe until the 1960s.

Before tackling the first part of this walk, download the Formby Civic Society guide (see website).

PATH OF THE NATTERJACK TOADS

'Birkdale nightingales'

Ainsdale Discovery Centre
The Promenade, Southport, PR8 2QB
0151 934 2961
greensefton@sefton.gov.uk
Merseyrail to Ainsdale, then a 20-min walk along Shore Road
By car, take A565, turn left along Coast Road, then left again at The Sands Hotel

While thousands of shoppers were enduring the Saturday retail experience of Liverpool ONE, in a ritual repeated up and down the country, we found ourselves in a small group at the Ainsdale Discovery Centre. Unless you have a horse box in tow, resist the impulse to pay a fiver to park on the beach; leave your car in the centre's free car park and enjoy 'the most important sand dune system in the British Isles' – a reputation guaranteed since the transformation of a 'protected' reserve at Aberdeen into the Trump International Golf Links. Reconnecting with his Gaelic heritage, the billionaire president claimed to be 'overwhelmed by the imposing dunes and rugged Aberdeenshire coastline' and immediately set about destroying them.

Luckily, Trump has yet to discover any Scouse genes and we already

have a perfectly good golf course at Formby Hall, so the rare species of natterjack toad, great crested newt, sand lizard, dragonflies, tiger beetles and plant life residing here are safe for the time being. According to our guide, John Dempsey, the dunes and pools (aka 'slacks') represent 'prime real estate' for those that share the habitat.

Natterjacks arrived over the land bridge from Europe and, following the Ice Age, adapted to life by the seaside after being stranded here. The dunes and slacks around Ainsdale contain about 40% of the UK population and represent the largest colony in the country.

Masters of multitasking, they spend the spring mating, spawning and singing their heads off. Consequently, they are known locally as 'Birkdale nightingales', while at the other end of the beach Scousers referred to them as 'Bootle organs' as they performed an eerie soundtrack to accompany the public hangings taking place at Kirkdale Gaol throughout the 19th century.

Natterjacks are a protected species but face a range of natural predators, including birds, foxes, hedgehogs and dragonfly larvae, so human visitors need to respect the area's Special Conservation status. For this reason, an organised trip is recommended.

Popular evening visits are arranged to witness the springtime amphibian orgies, while summertime walks allow you to monitor the progress of the offspring. We managed to spot a tiny natterjack female but, without a guide, you wouldn't know what you were looking for – a bit like shopping in Primark.

SEFTON SHIPWRECKS

Whisky Galore

Lifeboat Road car park, Formby, L37 2EB
0151 934 2961 or email greensefton@sefton.gov.uk
Merseyrail to Formby station, then a 15-min walk
By car, take A565, turn left for Formby Lifeboat Road. Pay & display car park

Perched on a picnic bench overlooking the vastness of Formby Beach, it is hard to imagine that the Sefton coast has claimed over 300 ships since the Middle Ages. Most are hidden for ever beneath the sands, but at low water the remains of 10 or more resurface. Used for target practice during the Second World War by blatantly poor marksmen, they are now protected sites.

The wrecks appear to be accessibly close but should only be visited on walks organised by Green Sefton or the National Trust. Even then, conditions are prone to change: our booked trip to the *Star of Hope* at Ainsdale had to be switched at the last minute as the *Star* had decided to stay put beneath the sands.

Instead we found ourselves in the Formby Lifeboat car park at some unearthly hour, with project officer John Dempsey waiting to check our attire before catching the low tide. From the beach, it was possible to catch sight of two wrecks in the distance and one painfully close by.

On the horizon, the *Pegu* ran aground during rough seas in 1939 with a cargo of whisky destined for Rangoon. Customs and Excise officers believed the poor conditions ensured the security of the moonshine below decks, but local fishermen conducted a separate 'risk assessment' and 'salvaged' the lot, then stashed it among the dunes. A towering silhouette on the skyline for 50 years, the *Pegu* was hit by a tug in 1987 and its iconic mast brought down.

Closer to shore, we got to within 800 metres of the *Ionic Star*, which is inaccessible because of a 5-metre-deep underwater moat created by the scouring action of the sea. Carrying a much-needed cargo of meat, cotton and fruit from South America, she ran into trouble in the dark in 1939. To get here, she had escaped the predations of the German warships and U-boats patrolling the Atlantic only to run aground within sight of home. Her Blue Star sister ship, the *Doric Star*, was not so lucky – she was sunk by the *Graf Spee* two months later.

The least dramatic of the three, but the most poignant, is the only one you can make contact with. The *Bradda* was shipping coal to Ireland during a storm in 1936 when she ran aground. The all-Manx crew made flares of their clothing to attract help but were swept overboard and only one survived. Standing by the mussel-bound remains in touching distance of the shore, the *Bradda* is a grim reminder of why this coastline has been dubbed 'one of the most dangerous for shipping in the country'.

FORMBY POINT FOOTPRINTS

'Time future contained in time past'

National Trust Nature Reserve, Victoria Road, Formby, L37 1JL
01704 878591
www.nationaltrust.org.uk/formby
Merseyrail to Freshfields (for Victoria Road) or Formby if you wish to start at
Lifeboat Road; both involve a good 15-min walk
By car, take the A565 and come off at the last roundabout going north (BP
petrol station). For Lifeboat Road (L37 2EB), take the previous junction (Tesco
Superstore roundabout)
To get the most out of your visit, download Alison Burns' PDF: www.academia.
edu/8297938/The_Prehistoric_Footprints_at_Formby and sign up for a
National Trust Tour

Walking along the beach between Lifeboat Road and Victoria Road, it's easy to miss the ever-changing terrain beneath your feet. To the trained eye, however, muddy outcrops on the beach reveal a transient treasure trove of preserved, semi-fossilised footprints of the animals, birds and humans that passed over the mudflats some 5,000 years ago.

Known to most people as an up-market development of modern housing with two golf clubs, Formby nestles on the Northern line between sand dunes and the A565. Apart from its Viking name and the world's first Lifeboat Station (see page 163), it appears devoid of any historical merit (although an 18th-century plan to construct an enclosed dock here rather than 16 km down the coast might have led to a different story).

This image was turned on its head in the 1980s when retired teacher Gordon Roberts began to investigate the ephemeral trails of footprints that appeared to shift with the ebb and flow of the tides. Almost by accident, his discoveries established Formby as a unique feature of the prehistoric record. Approximately 70 metres from the dunes, a parallel strip of partly hidden sedimentary mud stretches 4 km from Lifeboat Road to Gypsy Wood Path, breaching the surface of the beach in four main clusters. At first glance, these dark strips of mud could be mistaken for sewage, but embedded in the layers of silt is an ever-changing display of animal and human footprints laid down aeons ago.

During the big meltdown that followed the last Ice Age, rising sea levels began to reshape the coastline from Blackpool down to North Wales. Massive sand bars created lagoons into which rivers and streams deposited mud and silt on their rush to the sea. The resulting saltmarsh generated an ecosystem that our guide, Jamie Lunt, describes as 'a mosaic of different habitats and vegetation ideal for foraging herbivores and perfect for the hunter-gatherers who camped nearby. As they tracked their prey and foraged for shellfish, our Stone Age ancestors left evidence of the hunt: footprints of humans, wading birds, wild boar, deer and the mighty auroch were impressed into the sheltered mudflats to be baked hard by the summer sun. These were then sealed by layers of silt and buried for millennia beneath the shifting sands.

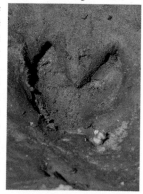

Recent encroachment by the sea and erosion of the sands at Formby Point (the dunes are receding at 5 metres a year) are stripping away the covering to expose discontinuous outcrops of marine sediment and, as the tide washes away the silt, the weather-hardened strata surrender their temporary secrets.

BRASS MERMAIDS
OF THE FISHERMEN'S REST PUB

Then when the storm howls loudest, pray of your charity
That God will bless the lifeboat, and the Warriors of the Sea

2 Weld Road, Birkdale, PR8 2AZ
01704 569986
fishermens.rest/index.html
Mon–Thurs 11am–11pm, Fri & Sat 11am–midnight, Sun 11am–11pm
Merseyrail to Birkdale station, then 10-min walk down Weld Road
Bus 47 from Queen Square to Weld Road, Birkdale
By car, take A565 coastal road, then right off roundabout before entering Marine Drive

Now a thriving gastropub near the coast at Birkdale, the Fishermen's Rest is all that remains of the very grand Birkdale Palace Hotel for which it served as a coach house.

A CAMRA award winner and TripAdvisor Certificate of Excellence holder, and voted one of Famous Grouse's 'Top 100 famous pubs in Britain', the 'Fish' is a family-friendly local with a cheerful atmosphere and occasional light entertainment, an ambience which belies the tragic story behind its name.

On the night of 9 December 1886, the *Mexico*, a German barque outward bound from Liverpool, ran aground on the Horse Bank off Ainsdale Beach during a full-blown gale. In heavy seas, the *Eliza Fernley* lifeboat from Southport and the *Laura Janet* from Saint Annes were launched to save the crew. The *Eliza Fernley* got to the stricken vessel first but capsized in the swell; 14 of the 16 crew were trapped beneath the boat and perished. Meanwhile, the boat from Saint Annes rowed out to the *Mexico* and hoisted sail. Red lights were seen from the beach but the lifeboat disappeared and was found the next day with three dead crew 'hanging from the thwarts with their heads downwards. Every man in the crew was lost.'

The 12 crew from the *Mexico* had lashed themselves to the rigging to survive and were eventually rescued by the *Charles Biggs* from Lytham which, on its maiden voyage, rowed across the Ribble estuary to the treacherous sandbanks to make good its first rescue.

To this day, the disaster remains the worst in the history of the Royal National Lifeboat Institution: 27 lifeboatmen were lost, leaving behind 16 widows and 50 orphans. The following day, the bodies of the crew were retrieved from the beach and transferred to a temporary morgue in the Palace Hotel's Coach House bar.

The hotel itself was used for the hastily convened coroner's inquest into the tragedy. In 1969, the Palace Hotel was demolished but the Coach House bar survived as a pub and was renamed the Fishermen's Rest in memory of that night; the 14 brass mermaids around the bar commemorate the lives of the Southport crew who perished.

Over 12 years, the *Eliza Fernley* was called out to 14 wrecks and saved 52 lives. A lifeboat station was erected to house her replacement and still survives 130 years on. This is now home to the Southport Offshore Rescue Trust, which runs an independent service to guard the coastline between the Mersey and the Ribble.

BRITISH LAWNMOWER MUSEUM

Enter lawnmower Valhalla

Stanley's hardware store
106–114 Shakespeare Street, Southport, PR8 5AJ
01704 501336
www.lawnmowerworld.co.uk
Mon–Sat 9am–5.30pm, closed Sun
Merseyrail to Southport station
Bus 300 from Queen Square
By car, take A565, 45 min from city centre to Lord Street
Walk (or drive) down East Bank Street and turn right at the roundabout.
Shakespeare Street is the continuation of St James Street

At first glance, Stanley's hardware store looks no different to any other independent DIY shop but, for a small fee, you will be admitted via a turnstile into lawnmower Valhalla, for here (hidden away upstairs) is the only lawnmower museum in the country.

Rightly referred to as 'the epitome of the uncommonly British attraction', this treasure trove is the brainchild of Brian Radam, a former apprentice at Atco and British lawnmower-racing champion. Despite having an allergy to grass cuttings, he has amassed a collection of over 400 machines, offering 'a unique insight into the fascinating history of the lawnmower'.

The lawnmower (never to be confused with the humble grass cutter) was invented by mistake: it started life in 1830 trimming the uniforms

of Guardsmen, but Edwin Beard Budding soon realised its potential for the English country garden and, to avoid local speculation regarding his sanity, tested it under cover of darkness. One of the earliest enthusiasts was Charles Darwin, who was the proud owner of a Samuelson Donkey. Later models were produced by Atco, Qualcast, Rolls-Royce, Hawker Siddeley and Dennis, but the most expensive is a solar-powered Husqvarna robot which cost £1m to develop and had a purchase price of £2,000 in 1995.

The lawnmower is related to several well-known sayings: 'Shanks's pony', 'horsepower' and 'in the slips' all originate from the early days of mower power, but if you want to know why, you'll have to visit the museum. Also revealed is the meaning of 'Money for old rope', the clue being that the official hangman, Albert Pierrepoint, was paid £15 for each hanging ... exactly what he paid in 1960 for the Jerram and Pearson lawnmower that he later donated to the museum. It is not possible, however, to link this purchase to the fee for a particular hanging as Pierrepoint resigned his post in 1956 – in protest at being shortchanged by the Under Sheriff of Lancashire for a hanging that was cancelled by a last-minute reprieve.

Other celebrity donations include Roger McGough's trowel, Nicholas Parsons' secateurs, Joe Pasquale's trimmer and a heavy metal mower donated by Brian May, which the rock star described as 'the Gilbert Harding of lawnmowers (suffering from) occasional bouts of severe indigestion and the bad humour that goes with it, yet struggling to be a useful member of society'.

THE MASTER BARBER'S SHOP

'Run by gentlemen for gentlemen'

Wayfarers Arcade, 315–317 Lord Street, Southport PR8 1NH
01704 807176
www.themasterbarber.co.uk
sales@themasterbarber.co.uk
Merseyrail to Southport station
Bus 300 or 47 from Queen Square
By car, take the A565 to Lord Street

Liverpool is woefully short of traditional barbers with the training and expertise to give you something for the weekend you would be proud of – for that kind of tonsorial experience, you need to travel to Southport. The Master Barber's on Lord Street focuses on the traditional skills of the

barber shop. Award-winning duo Robert and his son, Dan, have been here for eight years and dad has been in the trade for 56. He trained under World Champion Roger Poirier (personal barber to Edward VIII) and Vidal Sassoon, where he learned the art of precision cutting, hot towel shaves, singeing and neck massage. The issue of training and certification is one the shop takes seriously in an industry bedevilled by cowboys and low levels of qualification. From beneath Robert's clicking scissors, a regular agrees: 'Two bad experiences elsewhere – that's why I come here.'

Intrigued as a kid by the practice of singeing hair, I asked about its purpose. Theories include the prevention of bleeding (?), cauterising of split ends, promotion of conditioning, encouragement of growth by opening up the follicles and a neater finish. But Mr Poirier's answer, when asked the same question, is best: 'It puts another tanner in the till.'

'All women should be banned from barber shops'

Among the rash of Turkish barbers popping up across Liverpool, two parlours stand out.

Firstly, Liverpool's most famous:

In Penny Lane there's a barber showing photographs
Of every head he's had the pleasure to know.

A bit of poetic licence from Macca as the barber's is actually in Smithdown Place and the photos were of monochrome celebs sporting quiffs and square necks. It was known for years as Bioletti's. Old Man Bioletti cut John Lennon's hair and during the 1960s would send a crew armed with clippers to the Blue Coat School where, over two nights, 150 boarders were shorn (anyone caught dodging a short back and sides would be sent back the following week for 'Bioletti's revenge'). The shop ended up in the hands of Tony Slavin, who converted to Unisexism, and it's now in the hands of Adele Allan, who battled a rival on Penny Lane in 2010 to stake its claim as the original.

Second, and most notorious, is the provocative BarberBarber on College Lane. Billing itself as exclusively 'For Scoundrels & Gentlemen', it caused a stir when in 2014 it proclaimed it was a no-go area for women. Defending his men-only space as pro-men rather than anti-women, Johnny Shanahan won the Donald Trump Medal for Diplomacy when he announced, 'All women should be banned from barber shops.'

BAXENDELL ASTRONOMICAL OBSERVATORY

'The heavens declare the glory of God; and the firmament sheweth his handywork'

Hesketh Park, Southport, PR9 9JN
For Open Days and tours, see www.southportastro.org
Train to Southport station, then 20-min walk along Lord Street
Bus 47 from Queen Square to Hesketh Park or bus 300 from Queen Square to Lord Street
By car, take the A565 Coastal Road, then turn right off the roundabout at the end of Marine Drive

After years of neglect, the splendid Baxendell Astronomical Observatory has undergone a much-needed facelift and is once again open to the public.

Originally in the possession of Sir Thomas Bazley, the timber structure, which housed a 6-in. (15-cm) refracting telescope and German Equatorial Mount, was donated in about 1877 by Bazley to Joseph

Baxendell, local astronomer and head of the Meteorological Observatory in Hesketh Park. The gift was transported to the back garden of Baxendell's home in Liverpool Road, Birkdale (no longer there).

Following his death in 1887, Baxendell was succeeded by his son and the Baxendell family donated the observatory to the then Southport Corporation's Education Department. It was placed on top of a newly built brick structure with funds from the residual estate of the late John Fernley, a retired Cotton Spinner manufacturer and prominent Southport philanthropist and benefactor. The building has a couple of arched entrances while an original iron staircase to the rear provides access to the first floor. Inside the dome that houses the telescope – built in 1869 by the world-renowned manufacturers Thomas Cooke & Sons – is an inscription with the words of Psalm 19 ('The heavens declare the glory of God; and the firmament sheweth his handywork').

The observatory continued in sporadic use by local groups until the 1990s, when it ceased to function. Time has taken its toll and the rotting woodwork has been further compromised by an unfortunate attempt to restore it in 2008. The newly-added copper cladding proved so heavy that the track wheels gave up and the dome could no longer track the

movement of the moon but instead stared blindly in the direction of Ireland. During this expensive 'renovation', someone also decided that it would be a good idea to re-move the guttering from the dome – unsurprisingly, this resulted in a roof impersonating a sieve.

In 2017, with funding from Sefton Council, new contractors with the required skills in heritage projects undertook a major restoration. The observatory is now in the best condition since it opened nearly 117 years ago.

Floral clock

Donated in 1936 by an ex-mayor, the floral clock can be found in a garden down some small steps. Alongside is a small brick building which houses the clock's mechanism. It is thought that the floral clock is the only one left in a public garden still using its original mechanism ... which needs to be wound up by hand every day.

OLD BAKEHOUSE STUDIO

29

The first parson launched into space

Botanic Road, Churchtown, PR9 7NE
Bus X2 from Queen Square to Churchtown or train to Southport, then bus 44 to Churchtown
By car, take the A565, 50 min from city centre via Southport

A stone's throw from St Cuthbert's Church in the picturesque village of Churchtown, you will find a wooden shack mostly concealed by sprawling undergrowth; a plaque confirms that you have landed at the birthplace of Dan Dare.

In 1949, the Rev. Marcus Morris, wartime RAF chaplain and vicar of Saint James' Church Birkdale, wrote an article attacking the violent comics flooding into the UK from the US. His antidote was a comic for boys with wholesome characters and uplifting Christian principles. He teamed up with local artist Frank Hampson, to create the comic's superhero, billed (in the dummy) as Chaplain of the Interplanet Patrol and a cross between Biggles, Flash Gordon and Paul of Tarsus.

By the time the Hulton Press had agreed to support the magazine, the flying padre had lost his dog collar, and the *Eagle*, with Dan Dare at the controls, had landed. The first edition sold over 900,000 copies.

Hampson came up with the original ideas, epic storylines and stunning artwork, assisted by a team of illustrators and helped with the

odd storyline by the Rev. Chad Vara (later to found the Samaritans) and a young sci-fi writer by the name of Arthur C. Clarke. Hampson's cinematic eye and attention to detail produced technicolour work of the highest quality. To this day, it ranks among the best examples of graphic art anywhere, ever. Under his studio system, the *Eagle* was produced in this old wooden bakehouse with a corrugated iron roof before moving to Epsom.

Rev. Morris went on to pursue a parallel career in publishing along with 'an energetic and exotic love life on the side'. He launched the UK edition of *Cosmopolitan* in 1972 and ended up with an OBE.

Hampson, on the other hand, argued with his new publishers who forced him out of his studio in 1962, and retained copyright over his work. He subsequently forbade any mention of Dan Dare but was later forced to admit, 'Although I often wish he would, Dan Dare refuses to die.'

Hampson's influence on comics, TV, film and computer games endures and his admirers include Terry Jones, Stephen Hawking and Brian May. He also appears in the lyrics of David Bowie, Elton John and Pink Floyd. As teenagers, Gerald Scarfe (winner) and David Hockney competed for an Eagle art prize.

In 1975, Hampson was acclaimed Prestigioso Maestro by his fellow artists at an international convention in Lucca, Tuscany. He has plaques at his birthplace in Audenshaw and home in Epsom.

A permanent Dan Dare exhibition can be seen at Southport's Atkinson Museum.

30

ST CUTHBERT'S GRAVEYARD

The grave of a European slave

Botanic Road, Churchtown, PR9 7NA
01704 232139
stcuthbert.org.uk (see website for service times and events)
Bus X2 from Queen Square to Churchtown or train to Southport, then bus 44 to Churchtown.
By car, take the A565, 50 min from city centre via Southport

There has been a church on the St Cuthbert's site since the [...] century, but the one you see today dates from the 1730s, a few yea[...] after the interment of an unusual slave: in a grave behind one that is fenced off, to the right of the entrance, is the final resting place of Thomas Rimmer, who spent part of his life as a slave on the Barbary Coast. A brass plaque repeats the fading epitaph on the headstone, which reads, 'Here Lyeth the Body of Thomas Rimmer Mariner who was captive in Barbary sixteen years and six months who departed this life the Sixth of January the Sixty first year of his age in the year of our Lord 1713.'

In contrast to Liverpool's involvement in the slave trade, it is strange to be reminded by a grave, just up the coast, that Europeans could be the victims of slavery as well as profit by it. The Barbary corsairs were pirate raiders from North Africa who terrorised coastal settlements from the Mediterranean to the south-west of England and as far north as Iceland in search of human booty. During the 'sacking of Baltimore' in 1631, a raid on the Irish coast led by Morat Rais, a Dutch convert, captured 20 men, 33 women and 54 children who were sold at auction in Algiers.

Inside the church, the superb carved wooden reredos by Richard Prescott, transferred from St Peter's Pro-Cathedral in Liverpool (see page 13), can be admired, along with a window celebrating the Bibby family and the 'squire's pew' still used by the Hesketh family when in town. The chandeliers are a copy of those in the House of Commons. Against the churchyard wall are a set of stocks – a reminder of the power of 'bawdy courts' to punish all manner of sinfulness, including blasphemy, drunkenness and fornication. Offenders were sentenced to public humiliation in the stocks 'at the mercy of the mob', which often meant being pelted with excrement, dead vermin or the rotten veggie option but, if you were well liked, you might get showered with flowers or suffer having your feet tickled.

In or around 1860, Thomas Rimmer was recorded as the last man to be sentenced to the stocks at St Cuthbert's, having refused to pay a fine for drunkenness. History does not reveal whether Thomas got [p]elted with crap or had his feet tickled.

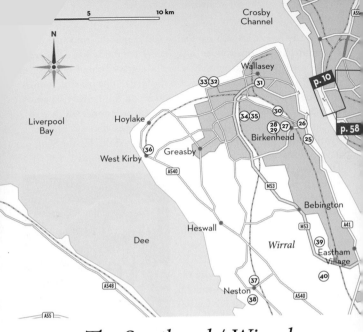

The Southend / Wirral

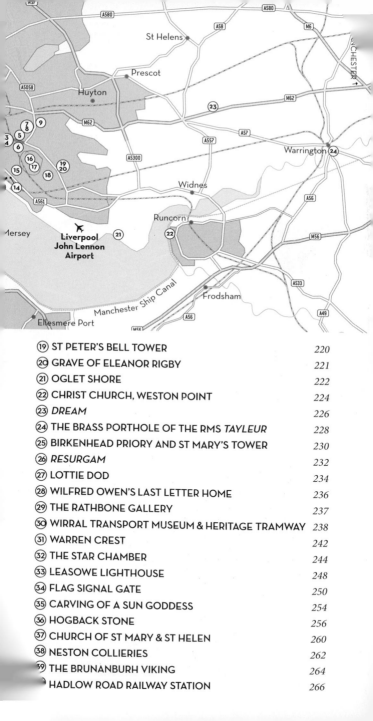

QUAKER BURIAL GROUND

A secret garden hidden from view

Arundel Avenue (opp. Halkyn Avenue), L17 2AT
www.tann.org.uk
Sun 1.30pm–4pm
Group tours may be arranged by phone: see website ('Landmarks' page) for
contacts
Buses 80 and 80A from Liverpool One bus station, then short walk from Ullet
Road
Or take any of the 86s from Liverpool One, then short and walk from
Smithdown Road

At the end of a narrow gated passage off Arundel Avenue lies a concealed burial ground maintained by a band of volunteers dedicated to its preservation as a garden. The site was originally purchased in the 19th century by Quakers who had been ordered by the Privy Council to vacate their city-centre cemetery on grounds of public health. The cemetery was closed and all the bodies exhumed. In 1861, they were reinterred at the new burial ground, which continued in use for the next century. At some stage a large section was sold to the Guardians of the Poor to enlarge the Toxteth Park Workhouse. The burial ground then became landlocked except for the gated entrance.

In keeping with Quaker notions of plain living, the uniform headstones exhibit none of the diversity and overblown detail found in the Toxteth cemetery next door. The information on all the headstones has an identical format and is restricted to the name of the deceased and a numerical reference to the date of death – so avoiding any names of months that honour false deities. As my volunteer guide Fran points out, 'Quakers would never permit the name of a pagan god or a Roman emperor to appear on a headstone – that would be heresy.'

Liverpool Quakers, however, seem to have been quite radical in even allowing headstones (at the Ormskirk cemetery, a grave is simply marked by a flat stone or no stone at all). Nevertheless, the placing of flowers of remembrance upon a grave continued to be frowned upon ... which is ironic given what the site has now become.

The final interment here took place in 1961 and, apart from the occasional use of the columbarium for cremation urns, the cemetery was then abandoned. In 2013, the plot was offered to TANN (The Avenues Neighbourhood Network) for allotments ... forgetting that, while the dead have no need of water, plants cannot survive without it. Despite this, the group have nurtured the legacy of wild flowers such as lady's smock, wild garlic and buttercups and transformed a graveyard into an inner-city meadow.

The grounds are now part of the National Gardens Scheme and recently received a donation from Elizabeth Rathbone, whose family were originally Quakers. On the day of our visit, an elderly couple from Yorkshire had turned up in search of their ancestors. 'We will be back soon,' they beamed. They had not yet found the evidence they were looking for, but perhaps they had simply discovered something else.

THE STAINED-GLASS WINDOWS OF ULLET ROAD UNITARIAN CHURCH

Revelations of the Arts and Crafts movement

57 Ullet Road, L17 2AA
0151 733 1927 or 07828 883484
philipunitarian@gmail.com
www.ukunitarians.org.uk/ulletroad/
Weekdays for various events
Church services: Sun 11am (please remember this is a place of worship, not part of a tourist trail)
For tours, contact Rev. Phil Waldron by email or phone
Bus 80 or 80A from Liverpool One bus station

Local people pass the Unitarian Church on Ullet Road every day of their working lives without realising that it was the fourth manifestation of the Castle Hey meeting house built in 1687 to cope with the overspill of dissenters from the Ancient Chapel of Toxteth (see page 202). The church is a revelation: a shared space that makes no distinction between nave and chancel. The stained-glass windows above the altar are by Burne-Jones, while those lining the nave were created for the new church by William Morris, as was the rose window over the entrance. For some reason, these fabulous Arts and Crafts creations have never been as well publicised as those featured at All Hallows' in Allerton.

In the evenings, the chancel is illuminated by chandeliers which hang like giant mistletoe above the pews. To the right of the altar stands a mobile wooden font designed by a relative of Beatrix Potter.

After an impressive art deco library with extensive murals, the tour enters an anteroom which houses the busts and memorial plaques transplanted from the old Renshaw Street chapel over 100 years ago – no sombre collection of epitaphs, but a celebration of the inspirational Unitarians who played such a dynamic part in the formation of modern Liverpool. Not content to sponsor a narrow Protestant ethic devoted to the spirit of capitalism, these were people who felt they had a mission to improve the health and well-being of local people – it reads like a roll call of Liverpolitan movers and shakers. But, for one in particular, it was personal: William Rathbone VI had been refused permission to marry by the Quakers and shifted allegiance to get his way.

A theological joke

At the main entrance, the architect has left his own theological joke: three vacant holes for bell ropes. As Unitarians reject the notion of a Holy Trinity, there is no point in bells representing Father, Son and Holy Ghost – a quick peek from the street reveals a redundant belfry.

SECRETS OF THE PALM HOUSE

The closest living example of what the Brontosaurus had for brekky

Sefton Park, L17 1AP
palmhouse.org.uk
15-min walk from St Michaels station or Mossley Hill
Any bus stopping on Smithdown Road, Croxteth Road or Aigburth Road

The Palm House in Sefton Park is a much-loved landmark but, if you know what you're looking for, there are some lesser-known treats in store.

In the days before David Attenborough and Gardeners' World, the only way the general public could experience exotic flora and fauna was by visiting a private zoo or botanical garden. In its day, Sefton Park and its Palm House attracted visitors from across the north-west as Liverpool made its mark as an early tourist destination.

The Palm House was built in 1896 by Mackenzie and Moncur (note the ornate letter 'M' above each entrance) at a cost of £12,000, with every pane of glass cut to a unique size – despite the impression of being curved, all the panes are flat. During the Second World War, the Palm House was camouflaged to look like parkland, but it lost all 3,710 panes during a night raid when a bomb landed close by.

Restored in 1951, it drew even closer to the brink of disaster courtesy of council neglect during the 1980s, only to be rescued by a group of volunteers (of course). The 'sponsor a pane' campaign triggered its magnificent restoration and it now hosts public events and private celebrations.

Among the botanicals, you will discover some obscure treasures.

At the base of the spiral staircase (now closed), the only surviving plant from the original collection – a huge palm nicknamed 'Palm Olive' after a stoic campaigner – is a species that has been around for millions of years. The Cycad is so old, it's referred to as the 'living fossil'. During the Mesozoic period, Cycads accounted for 20% of plants worldwide. This one, from the Cycadaceae family, evolved a mere 12 million years ago but is the closest living example of what the Brontosaurus had for brekky.

By the main entrance stands the Dracaena Marginata (Dragon Tree) from Madagascar which thrives in botanical retreats but is susceptible to red spider mite, thrips and scale insects. In this pesticide-free ecosystem, the plants are protected from such bugs by voracious wasp and ladybird larvae imported by post from Holland (close scrutiny reveals them at work).

The statue of *Highland Mary* by Benjamin Spence celebrates the young woman who was the love of Rabbie Burns' life; she died young and inspired much of his poetry. Beneath one of the statues lies a time capsule but, as no one can remember which statue, this is a real secret!

NEARBY
The Legacy Garden ④

Outside, the restored statue of Peter Pan is flanked by wonderful beds of perennials. The path dips to a lower level that rehouses stock from the now defunct Wildflower Centre, creating a striking Legacy Garden of cornflowers, poppies and wild daisies to remind us of what we have lost.

THE NO. 5 BUS INTO TOWN

*'There are places I'll remember ...
Some forever, not for better'*

It's no longer possible to get the Liverpool Corporation No. 5 bus from Menlove Avenue into town or the No. 4 detour via Penny Lane, Church Road and Picton Road to the Pier Head. But this is the route John Lennon and Paul McCartney used to take to college ... and to the clubs, cafes and record shops dotted about Liverpool where you could pick up the American music that was to influence the Mersey Sound.

Both buses stopped at the now famous Penny Lane terminus before going their separate ways. Several of the people and places around here made it into the lyrics of The Beatles' eponymous number one single in 1967 – fireman, barber, banker and 'a four of fish and finger pies' all contributing to the disc's suburban appeal. But back in 1964, John Lennon had already worked the two bus routes into a song.

Asked by a journalist why he didn't put something of his childhood into his songs, Lennon set out to do just that but found it intimidating:

'"In My Life" started out as a bus journey from Mendips [where he lived with his Aunt Mimi] to town. And it was ridiculous ... it was the most boring sort of "What I Did On My Holidays Bus Trip" song and it wasn't working at all.'

Catherine Marcangeli and Steve Shepherd have researched Lennon's struggle with the lyrics by comparing his first drafts (www.beatlesbible.com/ songs /in-my-life/lyrics-in-my-life02/) with the pared-down version that ended up in the hands of George Martin. They show how Lennon distilled his recollections of 'all these places which had their moments' into general feelings of affection and nostalgia without naming any of them.

But it's more than a nostalgic trip down memory lane, recalling 'people and things that went before'. The excised lines include places that had intense meaning for a teenage Lennon whose Dad never came home and whose Mum had only just come back into his life – they are memorials rather than memories. As the writers conclude, 'It is an obituary for the world that Lennon had lost ... [featuring] landmarks of his life [which] might have felt certain, defined and secure.'

In 1980, Lennon recalled 'In My Life' as his 'first real major piece of work'. An NME poll in 2015 saw it voted No. 2 favourite Beatle track of all time.

Places Lennon decided to forget

No. 5 bus route *(Take the 76 to Penny Lane, then any of the 86s into town)*

• Bus stop opposite Mendips – the stop that Lennon's mother Julia was heading for when she was knocked down and killed on 15 July 1958.

• 'Good Old Dutch' – a biker cafe with a serious jukebox (now a plumber's but still displaying the windmill).

• 'St Columba' – St Columba's Church, now Shalom Court sheltered housing scheme. Its tower still stands on the junction before Sefton General Hospital, where Julia died and Lennon's son Julian was born.

• 'Docker's Umbrella' – the dockside railway. Lennon's absentee father preferred the dockside pubs to the company of his son.

No. 4 bus route *(Walk from Penny Lane up Church Road, then take the 78 into town)*

• 'Picton Clock Tower' – marking time (see page 194).

• 'Abbey Cinema' (now a supermarket) – where the young John spent 'happy hours' with Julia and probably saw early rock'n'roll movies.

IRWIN'S MURAL

Spooky ads

2A Allerton Road, L18 1LN
Any bus to Penny Lane

Hiding behind St Barnabas Church, on the wall of what is now a betting shop, is a splendidly preserved tiled mural for one of John Irwin's many grocery stores – a reminder of a fading age of commercial art. Irwin was an Irish immigrant who set up shop in Westminster Road in 1874, promising 'value, variety and quality'. By the 1950s, the family chain had established over 200 shops with distinctive façades. Many featured adverts in terracotta or terrazzo for a business intended to last, but in 1960 the chain of 212 shops was sold to Tesco to kick-start its battle for world domination. The advert on Allerton Road, proclaiming the prize-winning quality of their butter, is probably the finest surviving example.

These faint reminders are known as 'ghost signs' and represent a window on an era of commerce that has all but disappeared. With the advent of computerised graphics, photography, machine-made lettering and mass-produced billboards, there is little call for this level of individual artisanship. Luckily, there are still people who seek to protect and preserve these works.

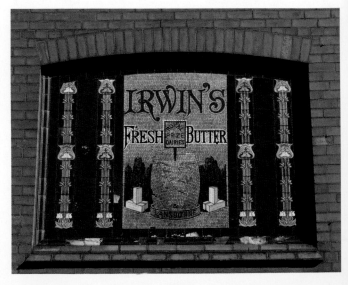

Other great ghost signs in Liverpool

The History of Advertising Trust (HAT) has a wonderful online archive of ghost signs (www.hatads.org.uk), with a fair proportion submitted from Liverpool by Caroline and Phil Bunford. They published the first book on the subject, *Liverpool Ghost Signs*, featuring local ads for Cooperative Societies, dairies, bakeries, booze and fags. One of their favourites is our John Irwin mosaic, but there are several other reminders of his empire (especially the terracotta facade on 95 Green Lane, L13 7BB).

Another terrazzo gem can be found at the junction of Eastdale Road and Wavertree High Street (L15 4HW), celebrating the work of the Toxteth Co-Operative Provident Society. The ultimate example, however, has to be the mosaic in the entrance to Fitwell's embroidery shop (276 Smithdown Road, L15 5AJ): the building was intended to be the Hatfield Hotel but, due to local resistance and objections from the landowner, the 3rd Marquess of Salisbury, it never had a guest or served a pint.

Other ghost signs mentioned in *Secret Liverpool - an unusual guide* include those relating to cowkeepers and dairies (see page 206) and Ma Noblett's toffee shop on London Road (see page 120).

According to Richard Gregory's excellent website (www.signpainting.co.uk), hand-painted signs publicising elections and gladiatorial contests already existed in Pompeii. Some have even survived the eruption of Vesuvius. In the 18th century, William Hogarth was not averse to earning a few bob painting signs, and the Victorian era became known as the Golden Age of English sign writers. Their work was displayed in fairgrounds, on barges and on public transport, but also on the walls of businesses and residential properties. According to the History of Advertising Trust (HAT), these painted signs (and more permanent murals and mosaics) were made to last, but over time they have faded alongside the memories of the people and products they sought to proclaim.

WAVERTREE LOCK-UP

One of Liverpool's two remaining lock-ups

Junction of North Drive/Mill Lane off High Street, L15 8JS
Buses 14/14A, 61/61A/61E, 78, 79/79D from Queen Square bus station

In the shadow of the famous Picton Clock Tower, on the city's only surviving patch of common land, stands one of Liverpool's two remaining lock-ups. Built in 1796 to detain local drunks, the aim was to save the expense of paying the neighbourhood constable 2 shillings a night to lodge them in his own home. Octagonal in shape but known

as 'The Round House', it was erected despite the objections of local toff John Myers, who claimed the scheme 'showed a desire to annoy him' by obstructing his view of the village green.

The lock-up was also occasionally used to quarantine cholera victims and destitute Irish families escaping the famine.

Close by the children's playground (once home to Wavertree Lake) stands the medieval sandstone archway marking the entrance to the Monk's Well. It bears a Latin inscription from 1414 which translates as: 'He who here does nought bestow, The Devil laughs at him below' ... a thinly veiled threat to those too mean to donate alms to the local monastery in return for a drink of water.

A pump was installed in 1834, but it was locked during Sunday services as it was feared that 'women met at the well when drawing water and stayed gossiping there'. The stone cross atop the base is a 19th-century replacement.

Following the introduction of piped water, the well became redundant, but it survived the development of a housing estate to become Liverpool's first Listed Building in 1952.

The other remaining lock-up can be found on Everton Brow. Nicknamed Prince Rupert's Tower, it has featured on the crest of Everton FC since 1938. In 1997, the club paid for its renovation and in 2004 illuminated it forever in blue.

NEARBY

Secrets of Wavertree High Street   ⑧

No. 102 High Street is Liverpool's only surviving example of a rare Georgian bow-fronted window. Home to various craftsmen over the past 200 years, including a wood turner who restored the window, the building is now Grade II Listed.

No. 95 High Street is the frontage of what was once known as 'the smallest house in England': 6 feet wide x 14 feet deep, it was home to a couple who raised eight kids there. One very large resident had to go upstairs sideways even after the staircase had been widened to 16 inches from its original 8! The 'house' was incorporated into the Cock and Bottle pub in 1952 and now acts as access to a four-bedroom apartment above.

No. 12 Arnold Grove, the plaque-free birthplace of George Harrison, is hidden away behind the pub off Chestnut Grove. A glacial boulder from Cumberland placed in front of Wavertree Library and known to generations of kids as a 'meteorite' gets a mention in George's autobiography.

LEPER'S SQUINT

Now you see me ...

All Saints' Church, Childwall Abbey Road, L16 0JW
0151 538 5973
www.allsaintschildwall.org.uk
Sun 10am for family service and 6.30pm evening prayer
Buses 14, 14A, 14B, 75, 79 or 79D to Childwall Valley Road

In the churchyard of All Saints' in Childwall (Liverpool's oldest surviving church), there is a reminder that in a bygone era the church overlooked a leper colony in Childwall Valley. Known as a leper's squint, or hagioscope, it was a mark of medieval social exclusion – a window that allowed lepers to observe church services from outside the building. Between the 15th and 18th centuries, the burial grounds were raised to cope with demand and outside access to the squint became partially

buried but can still be found at ground level behind the war memorial cross. However, it is best appreciated from just inside the entrance lurking behind the churchwardens' pew.

Despite the fear of contagion (both physical and spiritual), the

diseased outcasts were expected to attend church and confess the sins which, it was presumed, had dealt them such a fate. An arched recess allowed them to take turns via the squint without coming into contact with common and garden sinners in the congregation.

Other features of interest in All Saints' Church

Windows on the south side and the priest's door in the south wall date from the 14th century. There are clues to the church's even earlier origins in the fragments of Anglo-Saxon and Norman masonry in the west wall of the porch and a niche in the north chancel aisle.

None of the original stained glass survives, but the replacements, in conjunction with a good sunset, look spectacular as the evening draws to a close. In one of the alcoves off the south aisle, you can see some of the finest brasses in the North of England alongside a beautifully carved bench end from the family pew of the Norris's dating from the 16th century. The church also contains a good assortment of hatchments – lozenge-shaped coats of arms dating from the 17th century which also display other 'heraldic achievements' of long dead notables. Parish records reveal that the family of Anthony George, of Rainhill, can be traced back 12 generations to Thomas Wodley, who was born in 1543. This makes them, officially, Liverpool's Oldest Family.

Liverpool has two cathedrals, two football teams and three universities, so don't be surprised to learn that it is home to more than one leper's squint. The real deal may be in All Saints' Church but a representation on canvas also exists. After four attempts to win the John Moores Painting Prize, Michael Simpson had just about given up but, egged on by a persistent assistant, entered his 19th version of a squint in the 2016 competition: it is now a stunning painting on permanent display at the Walker Art Gallery, which bought it in 2017.

JOHN HULLEY PLAQUE

The founder of the Olympic Games

Steble Street Baths
Park Road Sports Centre, Steble Street, L8 6QH
Buses 82, 82c, 82d to Park Road

S teble Street Baths is the last place you'd expect to meet the founder of the Olympic Games but here he is ... and he doesn't look a bit like Pierre de Coubertin. Gazing back at you from a commemorative plaque on the wall is John Hulley. Liverpool born and bred and taught by Swiss

gymnast Louis Huguenin, Hulley invited international athletes to a public event called the Olympic Games the year before Coubertin was born.

A great believer in 'Muscular Christianity', he teamed up with like-minded health nut Charles Pierre Melly (see page 30), and in 1838 founded the Liverpool Athletic Club in Bold Street for the benefit of working men. (His attempts to introduce 'ladies' classes' were less successful and dismissed by outraged Liverpolitans as 'malignant activity'.) In 1865, the Liverpool Gymnasium moved to purpose-built accommodation on Myrtle Street. A remnant of the Myrtle Street gym frontage survived until the 1990s.

To drum up funding for the new gym, Hulley and Melly organised, in 1862, the first Grand Olympic Festival, which drew large crowds to the Mount Vernon Parade Ground. Two more games followed in 1863 and '64 (Coubertin was still in nappies), with another two transferred to Llandudno in 1865 and 1866. A year later, the final festival returned to Liverpool at the Myrtle Street gym and Sheil Park Athletic Grounds. According to Olympian Don Anthony, on the very day that Hulley chaired the inauguration of the National Olympic Committee in Liverpool, he was snubbed at the opening of his own gymnasium by Liverpolitans who thought he was 'no better than he should be'.

Hulley is buried in Toxteth cemetery, where his remains must be spinning like a top at the fate of his mighty Myrtle Street gymnasium ... let alone the media circus now passing itself off as the International Olympic Committee. His damaged headstone was rediscovered in 2008 and restored. The grave was rededicated the following year.

This summer a new statue to Hulley has been unveiled at the junction of Mariner's Wharf and King's Parade.

For more sporting heroes you've never heard of, please see following double page.

More sporting heroes you've never heard of ...

James Clarke: the first black man to have a street named after him

Not far from Toxteth cemetery is the Olympic-sized Picton Swimming Pool, where a plaque commemorates the achievements of James Clarke. At age 14, James stowed away on a ship leaving British Guiana for Liverpool. He was taken in by an Irish family from Scotland Road and worked on the docks. A keen swimmer, he joined the Wavertree Swimming Club and taught local children to swim. He rescued people from the Mersey and the Leeds and Liverpool Canal on many occasions and was decorated for his bravery; many of his medals can be seen in The People's Republic gallery at the Museum of Liverpool. It is claimed that, in 1986, he was the first black man to have a street named after him. James Clarke Street off Vauxhall Road is a stone's throw from the canal that made his reputation.

LOCAL HERO

WATER SPORTS CHAMPION

MULTIPLE LIFE-SAVER

THIS PLAQUE COMMEMORATES
JAMES CLARKE
BORN GUYANA 1885; STOWED AWAY ON A RUSSIA-BOUND SHIP; JUMPED SHIP IN LIVERPOOL 1899. CAMPAIGNED FOR SWIMMING TO BE ON SCHOOL CURRICULUM, SAVED MANY PEOPLE FROM DROWNING IN DOCKS, CANAL AND MERSEY. MEMBER OF WAVERTREE AND EVERTON SWIMMING CLUBS.
DIED LIVERPOOL 1946

PLAQUE UNVEILED BY
COUNCILLOR WARREN BRADLEY
LEADER, LIVERPOOL CITY COUNCIL
18 NOVEMBER 2008

Frank Soo: the only Asian ever to play for England

For fans too young to have seen him play, and even for people who don't care for football, Stanley Matthews is a legend. However, few have ever heard of his teammate at Stoke City in the 1930s who became the only Asian ever to play for England. The son of a Chinese father and English mother, Frank Soo grew up in West Derby and somehow escaped the clutches of both Everton and Liverpool to join a highly admired Stoke side that he went on to captain. In the words of author Susan Gardiner: 'In his time, [Frank] was regarded as one of the best by his fellow players, like Joe Mercer and Stan Mortensen, and it wasn't uncommon for Stoke City fans to say that Frank Soo was "better than Matthews".' Playing in the pre-video era and overlooked by Matthews in his memoirs, it is not surprising that Soo's memory has faded as the fans who did see him play make their way to the big Stadium in the Sky.

Max Woosnam: the greatest British sportsman

Max Woosnam, whose father was chaplain of the Mersey Mission for Seamen, was born in 1892 at 7 Riversdale Road, Grassendale (adjacent to Liverpool Cricket Club). He is regarded by many historians as 'the greatest British sportsman', but no one else has ever heard of him as he shunned celebrity. According to his biographer Mick Collins, 'He was an amateur sportsman and considered it the height of bad manners to talk about himself – he thought it was appalling vanity.' He won Wimbledon and achieved Gold and Silver medals in the 1920 Olympics, made a century at Lord's Cricket Ground, captained Manchester City in the 1920–21 season (despite being an amateur) and also captained the England football team.

Woosnam famously beat Charlie Chaplin at table tennis in a game where Chaplin had the advantage of a bat and Max handicapped himself with a butter knife! Chaplin sulked, so Woosnam threw the genius of comedy into his own swimming pool. Chaplin did not get the joke and they never spoke again. During the First World War, Woosnam served in Gallipoli and on the Western Front alongside Siegfried Sassoon. He blotted his copybook with Man City fans by acting as a 'scab' during the 1926 General Strike.

WILLS'S CIGARETTES

MAX WOOSNAM

ANCIENT CHAPEL OF TOXTETH

The oldest dissenting place of worship in the UK

Toxteth Unitarian Chapel, 371 Park Rd, L8 4UE
15-min walk from St Michaels station or bus 82/82D to Park Road
Services every other Sun 11am–12 noon; or by appointment with the caretaker
(0151 728 8028). Also open during Heritage Open Days

Behind a stone wall opposite the derelict remains of the Gaumont cinema is a hidden treasure with a Grade I Listing.

Four hundred years ago, Park Road was a babbling brook running through Toxteth Park to a picturesque dell (aka the Dingle), an isolated spot considered ideal for dissenters desperate to evade the constraints of the established church. A Puritan community settled here on land donated in 1612 by Sir Richard Molyneux (himself no stranger to religious persecution).

Six years later, a chapel was built and a bright 15-year-old preacher, Richard Mather, invited to serve as minister. Ordained to preach and trained to teach, he ran the chapel and the school. Appropriately, his star pupil turned out to be the most brilliant astronomer of his generation: Jeremiah Horrocks predicted the transit of Venus across the Sun and was an inspiration for Isaac Newton but died at the age of 23 (see the *Heaven & Earth* sculpture at Pier Head).

As an ordained minister of the established church, Mather's nonconformity got him into trouble and he fled to Bristol in 1639, then followed the Pilgrim Fathers to America. Cromwell attempted to join him but was stopped on orders of the King (not a clever move as it turned out).

Despite restoration work in the 18th and 19th centuries (including the demolition of the schoolhouse), some original stonework and internal features survive: a family pew bears the carved date (1650) of Mather's membership of the congregation and a clock by William Lascelles (1780) still keeps time opposite the pulpit. As a general rule, grave markers in the cemetery are simple, with very little ornamentation and not an angel in sight. However, cotton broker George Holt's tombstone carries a rather dynamic carving of a ship's anchor, while Elizabeth Gaskin's son enjoys an elaborate marble urn. If you search diligently, you may find a flying skull on the wings of a bat marking the grave of someone whose name has weathered away. The earliest gravestone still visible dates from 1723.

The Colybarium is a Who's Who of the city's most notable Unitarians, with memorials to Emma Holt (see page 210), James Rawdon, Charles Pierre Melly (see page 30), William Rathbone and daughter Eleanor.

Pilgrim Father

Richard Mather founded something of a religious and educational dynasty after reaching America. His son, Increase, became a preacher, a diplomat and the first president of Harvard. His own son, Cotton Mather, followed him into the ministry and was involved in the infamous Salem witch trials, which resulted in the execution of fourteen women, five men and two dogs (religious tolerance clearly did not extend to the practice of 'witchcraft'). Consequently, he was refused the presidency of Harvard and went on to help found Yale instead.

FLORENCE MAYBRICK'S POLICE CELL

'The English Dreyfus case'

The Old Police Station, 80 Lark Lane, L17 8UU
0151 728 7884
www.larklanecomcentre.org.uk
Merseyrail to Aigburth station, then across Aigburth Road
Bus 82/82D from Liverpool One bus station

At the back of the Old Police Station on buzzing Lark Lane can be found a 'two-minute wonder': a tiny museum devoted to a scandal which shook 19th-century England to its hypocritical core. The Police Station is now a community centre, but in 1889 it was the temporary home of a woman whose court case sparked a wholesale critique of the British legal system.

James Maybrick was a self-medicating oddball with a vivacious American wife, Florence, 23 years his junior and thought by some to be the most beautiful woman in Liverpool. Outwardly prosperous and happily married, they lived at the palatial Battlecrease House, 7 Riversdale Drive. In 1889, Maybrick fell ill and died in excruciating pain. His wife (who was having a fling with his chum, Alfred Brierley, at the time) was eventually accused of poisoning the cuckold with arsenic stripped from fly paper.

During the well-publicised trial, the judge seemed more impressed by Florence's morals than the flawed forensic evidence and, as Captain Halsey might have warned her, court cases in Liverpool do not go well for visiting Americans, dead or alive (see page 95). The judge, Sir James Fitzjames Stephen (Virginia Woolf's uncle), directed the jury to consider the 'horrible and dreadful thought that a woman should be plotting the death of her husband in order that she might be left at liberty to follow her own degrading vices.'

She was found guilty and given the ultimate penalty. A public outcry led to the sentence being commuted (and the judge having a mental breakdown). Florence was released after 15 years and returned to America, where she died alone having lost her son to poisoning when he mistook a cyanide solution for a glass of water (some people never learn).

James Maybrick was buried in Anfield cemetery and that might have been an end of it but for the discovery, in 1992, of a diary in Maybrick's own hand which showed that he was even more infamous as a criminal than a corpse – over a century after his 'murder', the man hit the headlines again as the self-proclaimed Jack the Ripper.

Ripperologists are divided over the authenticity of the diary: forensic scientists have branded it a fake, but at least one historian claims to be 'more than 90% convinced'. At an international conference in 1998, it was unhelpfully concluded that the 'fascinating' discovery was the 'work of a disturbed mind'.

BATTY'S DAIRY

'Once upon a time and a very good time it was there was a moocow coming down along the road'

Corner of Aigburth Road and Brentwood Avenue, L17 4LD
St Michaels station
Any bus along Aigburth Road

Next time you're buying a plastic pint in Tesco Metro on Aigburth Road, mosey along down for a reminder of how things used to be done: on the corner of Brentwood Avenue is a beautifully preserved carving above the door which records this as once the home of Batty's Dairy. The Batty family were farmers from Cumbria and belong to the history of Liverpool's forgotten cowkeepers.

It's hard to credit today, but in the era before pasteurised milk and refrigeration, the city's side streets had their own local dairy herds. Some had access to fields, parkland or the river, but many cowkeepers managed the whole process from a back yard.

Following a collapse of the rural economy during the mid-19th century, hill farmers from Cumbria and the Yorkshire Dales moved into the industrial centres to benefit from the huge demand for fresh foodstuffs. Farmers could send their milk in churns on the railway, but it was more convenient to move to the city and bring a few cows with them.

At its peak in 1900, there were over 4,000 cows crammed into the 900 cow-houses dotted across the city. Milking and bottling took place on the premises and orders of fresh milk and diary produce were delivered

daily to the doorstep. As green spaces were gobbled up for housing and supermarkets moved in, cow-houses closed and only a handful of dairies survived: Harper's said farewell to their 30-strong herd in the 1950s, while the Capstick family on Marlborough Road were probably the last in Liverpool to keep their own cows. A BFI cine film shows them being packed off to greener pastures in 1975 (player.bfi.org.uk/free/film/watch-leaving-of-the-cows-1975-online).

As author Dave Joy reminds us, these people have earned a special place in our heritage: 'They started out as farmers, adapted to become city cowkeepers and then adapted again to become suburban milkmen – part of the best doorstep food delivery service in the world and a key part of the British way of life.'

> ## Other cowpoke ghost signs
> Harper's Dairy on Rose Brae (L18 6JF), Hogg's on Little Parkfield Rd (L17 8UD) and The Old Dairy, McBride Street, Garston (L19 2ND).

> Doorstep deliveries in the UK are down from 89% in 1980 to 2.8% nowadays as supermarkets use milk as a loss leader and dish out body blows to dairy farmers and milkmen alike. Nevertheless, dairies still survive and, if you want to reengage with the daily clink of bottled milk and the tuneless whistling of the Great British milkman, deliveries are a mouse click away: www.mortonsdairies.co.uk/ or findmeamilkman.net

LIVERPOOL CRICKET CLUB PAVILION

'138 not out'

Aigburth Road, L19 3QF
0151 427 2930
www.liverpoolcricketclub.co.uk
Merseyrail to Aigburth station. Take a right on Mersey Road and a 5-min walk
to Aigburth Road, turn right and a 10-min walk
Bus 82 or 82A from Liverpool One bus station

The pavilion at Liverpool Cricket Club is hidden from all but its members as the building is concealed by the clubhouse and a wall running along Aigburth Road. It is, however, a magnificent extension overlooking a pitch that is second only in size to the Oval and venerated by such greats as Sir Donald Bradman, W.G. Grace and Wasim Akram. It is open to the public in the hope that visitors will take out membership. On a summer day, it is the ideal place to enjoy a cricket match and, if the weather turns, you can always take refuge in the pavilion bar. It has been home to LCC since 1881 and boasts 'the oldest pavilion at a first-class cricket ground', predating the stands at Lords and Old Trafford by 10 years and Trent Bridge by a little less. The ground's maiden first-class match was

between Lancashire and Cambridge University, and it has witnessed many a memorable game since as Lancashire's second home; in 2011, they won their first County Championship here since 1950 during the refurbishment of Old Trafford. In 1984, Gordon Greenwich hit his highest score for the Windies in a match watched by almost 8,000 spectators.

The ground has also hosted the odd football match – Everton played a couple of games here before ending up at Stanley Park. It was also home to the first England International to be played on Merseyside in 1883, when England trounced Ireland 7–0 in front of 3,000 fans in the return of a fixture the Irish had lost by a baker's dozen in Belfast the previous year.

The clubhouse has five squash courts in the basement and two bars named after former players who both won Victoria Crosses in the First World War (Noel Chavasse and Eric Dougall). Chavasse was an all-round sportsman and, along with his identical twin brother, represented Great Britain in the 1908 Olympics – both competing in the 400 metres. The Chavasse Cup (a mixed doubles tournament) is named in Noel's honour and competed for during the annual Liverpool International Tennis Championship, which now has its home at the cricket club.

Until 1975, the pavilion bore a warning that 'Dogs and Ladies Are Not Allowed' although, it seems, any old bloke was welcome – early members of the club were James Maybrick and his friend Alfred Brierley, who enjoyed very different roles in a sensational murder case (see page 204).

SUDLEY HOUSE

Aunt Emma's bequest

Mossley Hill Rd, L18 8BX
Train to Aigburth station, then 15-min walk up Barkhill Road
Bus 80 or 80A to Mossley Hill station, then 10-min walk

Built for Mayor Nicholas Robinson in the early 19th century, Sudley House became the home of the Holt family in 1884 – they stayed long enough to make a few alterations to the structure. Indoors, many of the period features remain, including the oak panelling, Lincrusta wallpaper and a marble fireplace sporting the family crest.

George Holt had been a serious collector of paintings and ceramics since the 1860s. In semi-retirement, he concentrated on acquiring a collection that reflected his religious sentiments and narrow appreciation of rural simplicity. The jazz musician George Melly (a distant relative) visited as a child and describes the place as 'furnished in restrained high Victorian taste'. He was charmed by the collection of paintings he

considered 'typical of the informed taste of the period'. They included works by Gainsborough, Reynolds and Landseer along with a handful of pre-Raphaelites condemned by one critic as 'twee, treacly and tearful'. Hardly a hothouse of the avant-garde, there is barely a female ankle to be seen, although Holt's purchase of a few Turners does him credit. It remains Britain's only surviving Victorian merchant art collection still hanging in its original location.

Holt's only child, Emma, inherited the place and lived there until her death in 1944. Melly recalls Aunt Emma in ambiguous terms: 'She was ... remarkably plain with a long face, incipient moustache and very small eyes ... It is possible she knew that it was unlikely she would be loved for herself alone and rejected any suitors ... Her character on the other hand was original and her generosity, especially to young people, unstinting.'

Clearly wary of mercenaries attracted to the family fortune, Emma became the 'fairy godmother' of Liverpool University Women's Hall, died unmarried and left Sudley House to the people of Liverpool. Thanks, Emma.

Tracing Turner - 'Light is therefore colour'

Sunsets over the Mersey can be glorious affairs, but there is no truth in the claim that 'the painter of light' committed any of them to canvas. According to Frank Milner (author of *J.M.W. Turner: Paintings in Merseyside Collections*), Liverpool was off Turner's normal route 'up North', although he did pass through the city on his way from Whalley Abbey to north Wales in 1799.

Robert Cadell's diary entries and sketches – discovered by Thomas Ardill and Matthew Imms in the Turner Bequest at Tate Britain – suggest that Turner may have travelled from Liverpool to Manchester on the newly opened railway. However, there are no sketches of Liverpool or its architecture in the archives, although his doodles of Fort Perch Rock and the Liverpool waterfront from New Brighton tell us he was definitely in the locality on his way to Scotland in 1831.

Whatever the artist's personal contact with the place, Merseyside is home to over 40 of his watercolours and oils. They were 'gifted' to the galleries by local collectors, thus avoiding the fate of those that ended up in private collections and museums abroad (Christie's flogged one in 2006 for $35.8m and Sotheby's netted $45m in 2010 for another).

Without the donation of these works, which allow us to appreciate the range of Turner's genius, Merseyside would have little to offer those in search of Britain's greatest painter. The Holt family, Sir Sydney Jones and William Hesketh Lever were the main players in putting together this legacy, which can now be traced to the following galleries:

Lady Lever Art Gallery (18 works): the major collection, which includes *Dudley*, 'an outstanding example of Turner's handling of the sublime' despite the tension between rural antiquity and forthcoming industrialisation.

Walker Art Gallery (10): in contrast to the encroaching steam power of *Dudley, The Falls of the Clyde* is a Romantic celebration of the dramatic power of nature that has Turner ignoring the largest mill in Britain blotting the landscape under his very nose.

Victoria Gallery & Museum (6): in his *Eruption of the Soufrière Mountains*, based on a sketch by Keane, Turner imagines what the erupting volcano may have looked like. Despite its poor condition, this oil painting remains a powerful reminder of the master's skill.

Sudley House (4): two oil paintings by Turner hang on opposite sides of the dining room. Although *The Wreck Buoy* was poorly received by critics, Ruskin claimed it was the last oil Turner painted 'before his noble hand forgot its cunning'. Turner had hoped that *Rosenau* would win him royal patronage – he was to be disappointed.

Williamson Art Gallery (3): Ruskin claimed that *Bay of Naples (Vesuvius Angry)* was his first encounter with Turner's work: he later added it to his own collection.

By public nomination, Turner's self-portrait has been selected as the new face on the £20 note, displacing Scottish skinflint Adam Smith. Tracy Emin was delighted: 'It's so amazing that an artist has been chosen for the £20 note, and an artist who was a wild maverick.'

Bank of England

"Light is therefore colour"

Twenty Pounds

Joseph Mallord William Turner (1775-1851)

©The Governor and Company of the Bank of England 2016   BANK OF ENGLAND

CALDER STONES

'Here and there, a well-turned scroll'

The Reader (International Centre for Shared Reading), Calderstones Mansion House, Calderstones Road, L18 3JB
Park open all year
External viewing: Winter 8am–5pm, Summer 8am-8pm. Mansion House entry 10am-4pm
Buses 75 or 76: alight at Crompton's Lane
By car, a 15-min drive from city centre. Free parking

At the centre of the park bearing their name, the Calder Stones have recently been incorporated into the lovingly refurbished Mansion House. Restored and encased in a glazed conservatory with turfed roof, they have finally been treated to the care they deserve. Considering that they are the city's oldest relics and the surest link to Liverpool's pagan past, the Calder Stones have been pretty shabbily treated over the years.

It is assumed that the stones started life as part of the internal decoration of a burial chamber and – like the complete versions found in Anglesey and Ireland – are 'passage graves' signposting the route to the spirit world of the incumbent's ancestors. The considerable effort involved – with detailed cups and circles engraved on them by Neolithic artisans – indicates they were significant burial structures rather than idle doodles for the amusement of the living; probably early attempts by preliterate humans to provide a meaningful response to the mystery of death.

For the next 5,000 years, the stones slumbered in obscurity until they cropped up in a 16th-century boundary dispute between the inhabitants of Wavertree and Allerton. By the 1820s, they had fallen into the hands of a J. M. Walker whose main priority seems to have been not to have to look at them – achieved by rearranging them at the entrance to his estate in a 'druidical' circle.

In the 19th century, the stones were celebrated in a poem by William Roscoe (a historian and leading abolitionist, see page 106) as 'the silent tomb, of ancient hunter or of tumulus, of warrior bold'. However, they were castigated in a letter to the local paper as a thorough disappointment save for 'here and there, a well-turned scroll'. At some point the burial chamber was consigned to the dustbin of history when burial remains discovered in the original grave were destroyed and the site was lost for ever.

The stones fared little better in the 20th century, when the circle became a decorative feature on a traffic island at the park entrance. In 1954, the 'corpy' (Liverpool Corporation) had them removed to its Garston depot, where archaeologist Forde-Johnson lovingly restored them using his toothbrush. After 10 years' careful flossing, they were returned to the park at the entrance to the Botanical Garden (widely regarded as second only to Kew), where they were padlocked inside a grimy and vandalised Perspex box. The Reader Organisation has done a grand job of rehabilitating the stones – the least you can do is drop by.

ALLERTON OAK

An old tree, a theatre and three dead horses

Calderstones Park, L18 3JB
24/7
Buses 75 or 76: alight at Crompton's Lane

A short walk from the Calderstones Mansion House takes you to a grand old oak tree purported to be 1,000 years old. It is fenced off to deter young monkeys who might seek to climb it or dogs that might cock a disrespectful leg. In the Middle Ages, before the building of courthouses, such iconic landmarks were often used to conduct local justice under the jurisdiction of a high constable appointed to keep his local Hundred in order. (A Hundred was the subdivision of a county, loosely organised around 100 resident freeholders.) A helpful noticeboard proclaims that the Allerton Oak was the meeting place of the West Derby Hundred, although some sceptics doubt the tree has been around for more than 600 years.

Having avoided destruction during a storm in 1701, the oak was less lucky in 1864, when flying debris from an explosion on the *Lotty Sleigh* – a barque carrying gunpowder on the Mersey – is said to have caused a split right down the great trunk. (As the river is over 1.6 km away, this is probably another local myth.) Whatever its history, the tree is a reminder that people lived and worked here well before Liverpool made its entrance on to the world stage. During the Second World War, families would send leaves and acorns from the tree to their soldiers at the front as tokens of love and good luck.

Fearful for the tree's future, the park gardener, John Warren, planted an acorn from the tree in 2007 which is well on its way to becoming 'Allerton Oak the Younger'.

The grave of three horses

The grounds of the Mansion House also contain a 1940s art deco-style open-air theatre, a ha-ha (brick-lined ditch to keep grazing animals from the front lawn) and a headstone marking the grave of three horses belonging to the Walker family – pits for paupers; headstones for horses.

NEARBY

The Ornamental Gardens are home to the final resting place of a remarkable dog. Jet of Iada was born nearby at the outbreak of the Second World War and was the first dog trained in search & rescue. Following his heroics during the London blitz, Jet became the first dog to be awarded the Dickin Medal (the animal equivalent of the Victoria Cross) and the first to be involved in a mining disaster. After leading the Civil Defence Section of the Victory Parade in London in 1946, Jet retired from active service. Fittingly, this local hero was the first dog in the UK to be buried in a public park with full civic honours. That's a lot of firsts!

ALLERTON TOWER PARK

18

Hidden gem

Woolton Road, L25 7UL
Bus 76 from Liverpool One bus station (alight at end of Menlove Avenue)
By car, take the A562 to the junction with Allerton Road (limited parking outside the entrance)

Despite being officially named 'Allerton Towers' by Parks & Gardens, there was only ever one tower: it adorned the Italianate mansion erected here in 1849 by a descendant of Liverpool's most prosperous slave-trading family to a design by Harvey Lonsdale Elmes (St George's Hall). Hardman Earle was a railway magnate who bought the 32-hectare site to show off his good fortune.

Several streets and a town bear the family name, but this was Harvey's crowning glory and served the family until 1928, when it was demolished. The family firm had offices at what is now the Hanover Hotel, 55 Hanover St, L1 4AF.

All that survives of the original mansion is the Orangery, which has remained almost intact alongside a stable block and bachelors' cottages that have not fared so well. The grounds are served by an underground stream providing the trees and shrubbery with a constant supply of water.

A walk with Richie the Ranger reveals arboreal gems that the average punter would otherwise miss, such as an evergreen oak, a perfect example of a Chilean pine (monkey puzzle), a 1,000-year-old yew tree and – unique to Liverpool parks – a hedgehog holly (opposite the lodge designed by Elmes which is still standing). Look out for a beautiful walled garden with a laburnum and wisteria tunnel and the old orchard, which

has a single apple tree still bearing fruit. 'Hidden gem' is an overused phrase, cheapened by its constant appearances on TripAdvisor, but this place deserves the accolade.

One ghost, two stories

Behind this glorious landscape lurks a spooky tale – well, two actually – possibly inspired by the same ghost. According to Liverpool ghostbuster Tom Slemen, a local maid from a nearby tavern (very dodgy) was impregnated by Hardman Earle's youngest son. Under threat of blackmail, the older brothers murdered the girl and dumped her down a nearby well.

Another story tells of a young servant girl getting herself in the family way courtesy of a guest at the manor who had little interest in playing Happy Families. In despair, she threw herself into a pool and drowned – she is alleged to be buried where the footpath and bridle way cross.

Either way, a ghost is said to appear dripping wet before gliding off. This would be no more than Shiverpool tittle-tattle were it not for Richie's claim that he witnessed the apparition along with two other park rangers. Hang around the back of the old stables and you might get a fright; if so, ask the spook which tale is true.

19

ST PETER'S BELL TOWER

Ringing the changes

Church Road, Woolton, L25 5JF
www.stpeters-woolton.org.uk
Open to genuine visitors/potential recruits Fri evenings (7.30pm–9.30pm)
Buses 75 or 76 from Liverpool One or 78 from Queen Square
By car, take the A562 (Menlove Avenue) and turn left at lights by Allerton Towers

T he 27-metre-high bell tower of St Peter's Church contains a small belfry that is usually closed to a general public largely unaware of its link to Woolton's place in musical history: in this cramped little space, a teenage John Lennon tried his hand at bell ringing. Predictably, he was

dismissed for 'behaviour not conducive to learning to ring properly' and went on to pursue a different musical career.

In July 2017, as part of the 60th anniversary celebrations of the 1957 Woolton Fete (at which chubby choirboy Paul McCartney first met a John Lennon reeking of beer), St Peter's Church and its hall were open to the public. This included a rare trip up the bell tower, to the chimes of 'Nowhere Man' (that's a call-change sequence of 441 234 5533 456 77 55 678 77 88 on St Peter's peel of eight bells).

On this occasion, the Tower Master, two sprightly accomplices and a Beatle nut all the way from the States keen to pull on Lennon's old bell rope are already in full swing. As boss of the belfry, Nick Willasey is the man responsible for stirring village locals from their Sunday morning sloth, but today he is showing us the ropes and, after a quick round, he assures us that we have what it takes to make the first team. I'm pleased to hear that I'm a 'natural' at something, only to realise that the man is on a recruitment drive: like Lennon, contemporary teenagers have other things on their minds at the weekend.

This is not a new problem: when the present church opened its doors on 8 September 1888, they had to borrow a team from St Peter's Liverpool to do the honours as they had yet to train up their own. The following month, the first full peal (of eight bells) shattered the peace and went on for 3 hours 28 minutes ... and they've been at it ever since. Not content with this, there are plans afoot to add two more bells. This will require a bigger team. So if you're a local with time to spare, get along to the clock tower on a Friday evening and try your hand at outdoing John Lennon.

Chief photographer at the *Echo*, and a man with a keen eye for architectural detail, Neville Willasey was forever telling his son Nick to 'look up' so that he might admire the work of Victorian architects and craftsmen. So it was something of a surprise to discover that Nick spends most of his time with raw recruits instructing them to do the opposite. 'Don't look up, there's nothing to see,' he says as your eye instinctively follows the snaking bell rope on its return through a hole in the ceiling.

The original bell tower was transported to Madeira when the church was rebuilt.

NEARBY

Grave of Eleanor Rigby

The grave of one Eleanor Rigby is in the church graveyard, but McCartney has always denied any connection to the song.

OGLET SHORE

A Site of Special Scientific Interest

2Oglet Lane, Hale, L24 5RH
*Buses 500, 80A, 86A to John Lennon Airport (get off at Dunlop Road and walk
to Dungeon Lane)*
*By car, take the A561 then the turning to the airport. Turn left along Dunlop
Road towards Hale and then a right turn down Dungeon Lane*
On foot via the Mersey Way (from Hale Lighthouse or Garston)

Hemmed in by industrial development, a housing estate and John Lennon Airport, Oglet Shore is a stretch of salt marsh on the north bank of the Mersey that still manages to attract a vast array of wildfowl, ornithologists and those craving an escape from the urban jungle.

Behind the airport, Dungeon Lane winds its way through fields to the still operational Yew Tree Farm. Directly opposite is an overgrown path down to Oglet Bay. This was once a small hamlet for farm labourers, but after the building of an overspill estate at Speke, the shoreline became a popular destination for families looking for some raw sewage to frolic in. The airport may carry John Lennon's name, but it was George and Paul who grew up in this bucolic haven. 'This is what I was writing about in "Mother Nature's Son",' admits Paul. 'It was basically a heartfelt song about my child-of-nature leanings.'

The idyllic shoreline may have inspired the line 'Swaying daisies sing a lazy song beneath the sun', but more recently this deserted stretch of the Mersey Way has become a paradise for 'Offroaders' and fly tippers and is also the inspiration behind a campaign to protect the SSSI from encroachment by the airport.

Dungeon Salt Works

Historically more significant than Oglet Shore is the stretch of beach at the end of Dungeon Lane. Near 'Dragon's Teeth' tank traps laid during the Second World War, the shoreline curves all the way to Hale Lighthouse and at low tide is a good walk. Slightly to the right are the remains of a harbour wall dating from 1697. This was the landing stage for rock salt mined in Cheshire and shipped across the Mersey to be refined here prior to being stored at the Salthouse Dock (1753) for export.

Salt was originally produced through evaporation by heating brine in huge pans. Cheshire, with its handy access to seawater and trees, became the undisputed centre of British salt production until the forests had been exhausted. The cost of transporting coal as a replacement fuel was prohibitive. This prompted a not-so-bright spark named William Marbury to sink the family fortune into prospecting for coalfields in Cheshire; he went bankrupt, having hit nothing but rich veins of rock salt.

Before long, others were making huge profits from mining local salt and the government invested heavily in a network of canals linking the Mersey to the coalfields of Lancashire, the salt mines of Cheshire and the docks and refineries of Liverpool. Writer Mark Kurlansky reminds us: 'The salt industry, the coal industry and the port of Liverpool fed off each other and together grew prosperous.' The sandstone harbour at Dungeon is one small remnant of this colossal trade.

Used extensively in the Nova Scotian cod grounds from the 18th century and exported around the world, salt mined in Cheshire became known as 'Liverpool Salt'. The town of Liverpool, NY probably derives its name from a contrived association with this global brand. According to the local librarian, the refinery town took the name either in honour of its namesake or as a marketing ploy.

CHRIST CHURCH, WESTON POINT ㉒

*The only church in Europe to stand on
an uninhabited island*

*The Port of Weston, Runcorn, WA7 4HN
Only way to get (legal) access is by taking the Mersey Ferries 6-hour trip, which
passes by the church. Cruises run April–Oct from Seacombe/Pier Head or
Salford Quays:
www.merseyferries.co.uk. See Brian Simpson's useful summary:
briansimpsons.wordpress.com/2017/05/31/manchester-ship-canal-cruise*

Deconsecrated and derelict (and closed to the public), Christ Church
stands within the Stobart Group's 'inter-modal port facility' aiming
to transfer freight from congested motorways to rail and waterway – a
19th-century solution to a 21st-century problem they did much to create.

The only way to appreciate the abandoned husk, and the 58-km masterpiece of Victorian engineering which sealed its fate, is to take the Snowdrop on one of its trips along the Manchester Ship Canal. Sandwiched between the M56 and M62 motorways, this hidden waterway tells the story of the long-running feud between the north's two great cities and the ongoing process of reinvention that has ensured its survival.

Manchester may have been King Cotton but Liverpool controlled the cotton trade, with tariffs reflecting its monopoly. So in 1882, engineer Daniel Adams proposed a 26-ft-deep (8m) canal wide enough to take ocean-going vessels from the Irish Sea, along the Cheshire bank of the river to Salford Quays. Although the scheme was derided by the *Liverpool Post* as 'throwing £10m into a big ditch', the first sod was cut by Lord Egerton at Eastham in 1886 and, employing 17,000 navvies (on 4½d per 10-hour day), it was completed in six years. Rising 60 ft (18m) from sea level through five locks, it passes beneath a series of swing bridges and the only 'swing aqueduct' in the world. The stunning Weaver Sluices continue to regulate the water levels.

But this is more than a museum – the industrial corridor has reinvented itself: refineries, chemical plants, flour mills, power stations and scrapyards pockmark a landscape that retains patches of rural serenity. Domestic animals graze the marshlands, migrating birds come and go, swans glide by and herons flap overhead.

Manc's revenge

At Davyhulme, four giant 'sludge hoppers' remind us that, in the late 19th and early 20th centuries, Manchester used to transfer its sewage here to be treated and pumped onto barges which then dumped it on Liverpool's doorstep.

Cheshire salt has been a traditional export since the 17th century (see page 223). In the 1700s, barges transported the stuff from the mines at Winsford along the River Weaver Navigation to the Mersey. In 1839, a knackered workforce petitioned the Trustees for the right to a rest on the Sabbath. To ensure that the bargees did not spend the day in the alehouse, three churches were built en route, Christ Church being the last on a headland above the Mersey.

Canal developments either side of the river have effectively cut the church off from its natural congregation and ensured its unique status.

DREAM

23

'From the earth comes light'

Sutton Manor, St Helens, WA9 4BE
www.dreamsthelens.com
Train from Lime Street to Lea Green, then a 20-min walk or buses 33 and 33a
from the station
By car, take M62 Jnct 7 A57 and turn left onto B5419. A short walk from
Sutton Manor car park

On the horizon above the eastbound M62 hovers an ambiguous shape. To discover its identity, you'll have to leave the motorway and head for Sutton Manor. Standing 20 metres high and weighing in at 500 tonnes, *Dream* is a concrete sculpture coated with glitzy dolomite that represents the head of a child of the new millennium. We are encouraged to imagine what the hopes and dreams of a 9-year-old girl in the post-industrial age might be. According to the artist, Juame Plensa, 'When I first came to the site, I immediately thought something coming out of the earth was needed. I decided to do the head of a 9-year-old girl, which represents this idea of the future. It's unique.'

However, the publicly funded Big Art Project required the support of the Steering Group, including a posse of ex-miners. As the artist felt they were not quite ready for conceptual art, he offered them a giant miners' lamp instead, entitled *The Miner's Soul*. Thankfully, this flirtation with the mundane was roundly rejected as a clichéd reminder of the nightmarish past rather than a beacon of hope for St Helens' future. The Sparkly Head, however, ticked all the boxes and was enthusiastically endorsed as 'a symbol of the area's post-industrial transformation'.

In *Ghost Milk*, Iain Sinclair's Ballardian assault on the Grand Projects of Regeneration, art installations such as the Angel of the North are dismissed as 'attractions brought into existence with the death of industrial process [icons] for a new theology of regeneration. The first religion to create its idols in advance of its doctrine. Construct your strange gods and we will invent the myths to explain them.'

Well, we've had seven years to think about it ... so what explanations can be offered and, more to the point, what is this local 17-year old dreaming about now? Has St Helens' post-industrial restoration already been realised 3km further along the M62 in the vast off-motorway storage depots on the old USAF airbase at Burtonwood? Is this where her future lies? Or does she have dreams of escape in which the motorway offers another way out?

THE BRASS PORTHOLE
OF THE RMS *TAYLEUR*

24

The Victorian *Titanic*

Warrington Museum and Art Gallery, Museum Street, WA1 1JB
http://wmag.culturewarrington.org
Weekdays 10am–4.30pm, Sat 10am–4pm
Train from Lime Street station to Warrington Central, then a 7-min walk
Bus 7 from Queen Square to Warrington bus station, then a 7-min walk
By car, take the M62 Jnct 9 A49. Car park behind the market

In Warrington Museum's Cabinet of Curiosities, a salvaged brass porthole reveals a tragic, unknown aspect of the town's past: sixty years before the *Titanic* set out on its doomed maiden voyage, the White Star Line chartered another disaster-waiting-to-happen in the form of RMS *Tayleur*. Constructed in the Warrington shipyards in 1854, this was bigger than anything built by Cammel Laird and sailed from Liverpool packed with mainly Irish immigrants hoping to make a new life in the Australian Gold Rush (most locals are unaware that Warrington had its own flourishing ship-building industry or that the vessel ever existed).

According to author and researcher Gill Hoffs, the vessel left port with several known defects. Unstable, overcrowded and unnavigable by virtue of an iron hull which played havoc with the compass readings, it was also rendered helpless in an emergency by an undersized rudder, unseasoned rigging and too few lifeboats. Within 48 hours, it ran aground on the island of Lambay, 8 km off Dublin Bay. Thinking they had arrived in Australia, the children rushed on deck only to discover the grim truth. While most of the men scrambled to safety, almost all the women (burdened by the fashions of the day) and all but one of the children perished. Four hundred lives were lost and Warrington's flirtation with shipbuilding was over. Parallels with the plight of today's 'boat people' are all too obvious.

Recently, divers on the wreck have salvaged an eerie consignment of blank gravestones being exported to the colony for those expecting to die on land.

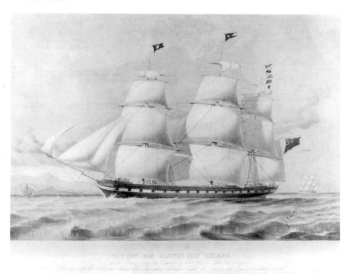

While you're there, be sure to pay your respects to the Woolston seal, who made it this far up the Mersey in 1908 only to be shot, stuffed and mounted so that local children could see what one looked like.

25

BIRKENHEAD PRIORY
AND ST MARY'S TOWER

*A monastery with no monks and a church
with no parish*

Priory Street, Birkenhead, CH41 5JH
0151 666 3537
thebirkenheadpriory.org
*Wed–Fri 1pm–5pm (12 noon–4pm in winter), Sat & Sun 10am–5pm (10am–4pm
in winter). Closed Mon & Tues, including Bank Holidays. Free admission*
10-min walk from Hamilton Square or 15-min walk from Woodside Ferry Terminal

Cut off from the parish once served by St Mary's Church, the site of
the oldest building still standing anywhere on Merseyside is tucked
away between dockside cranes, industrial units and approach roads to
the Mersey Tunnel. The restored priory houses a museum showcasing
monastic life behind which it is possible to access St Mary's Tower.

Founded around 1150 on 'a headland of birch trees' (hence the town's
name), the Benedictine priory served a remote hamlet, gave shelter to
travellers and operated the first ferry service between Cheshire and
Lancashire from 1318.

Close to the Welsh border and within striking distance of the Irish

Sea, Birkenhead's strategic
position ensured special
protection from the Crown.
The Mersey provided fish
and oysters for the table
and the priory lands were
farmed by the monks or
rented out. Travellers paid
for hospitality and the
ferry charged an exorbitant
1d (2d with horse) per
crossing. The local nobility
also paid the monks to
pray for their souls. There
were never more than
16 residents at any one
time. Career development
appears to have been a
haphazard affair: one prior
was pronounced insane
while another managed to

climb the greasy pole despite a conviction for murdering an Augustinian friar. The only surviving memorial commemorates Prior Thomas Rayneford (d. 1473) and can be found lying behind the altar rail in the chapter house.

Following the Dissolution of the Monasteries between 1536 and 1541, the estate (with an annual income of £19) was purchased for £568.11s.6d by the Worsley family, who maintained the chapter house but allowed the priory to become derelict.

The industrial foundation of Birkenhead led to a massive growth of population: from 110 in 1800 to 110,000 a century later. To cater to these souls, St Mary's was constructed here in 1822 as the town's first parish church. It survived until the 20th-century development of the area sounded its death knell – the Queensway Tunnel cleared out most of the local residents while the expansion of Dry Dock No. 5 into the churchyard removed many of the dead congregation.

The church was closed in 1974 and partly demolished, but the tower was spared, given a Grade II Listing and restored between 2013 and 2015. The result is a stunning 100-step building with, arguably, the best views of the Liverpool waterfront. Close to the top of the stairs, a window overlooks Dry Dock No. 4 where Laird's built the infamous *Alabama* (destined for the Confederate States Navy) in secret in 1862. If you have a head for heights, continue to the tiny rooftop, which will take your breath away ... along with any hat you may be daft enough to wear.

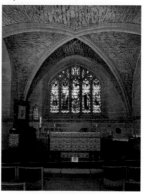

The tower is also a memorial to one of the few naval vessels ever to have been sunk twice. The submarine HMS *Thetis* sank during trials in 1939 with the loss of all but four of those on board. Refloated on the day war was declared, she was repaired and renamed HMS *Thunderbolt*. The name change did not improve her luck and she went down off the Sicilian coast with the loss of all hands in 1943. Each step of the tower carries a plaque bearing the name of a victim of the first tragedy.

RESURGAM

'If you want a submarine, we've got one to spare'

Woodside Ferry Terminus, Seacombe, Birkenhead, CH41 6DU
Best to come by ferry from the Pier Head
Make sure you don't miss the last ferry from Woodside or you're in for a painful detour by bus and train back to Liverpool!

In the car park behind Woodside Ferry Terminus, a surprise awaits you: a reconstruction of the world's first motorised submarine. It was designed by a Manchester clergyman and built at Birkenhead by Cochrane & Co. in 1879 at a cost of £1,538 (over £103,000 at today's prices). The *Resurgam* was constructed from iron and wood with a steam-driven propeller and was operated by a crew of three. Following successful trials, she was escorted from Birkenhead for a demonstration to the Royal Navy at Portsmouth but only got as far as Rhyl, where the escorting vessel got

into trouble. In the ensuing confusion, the submarine nosedived out of naval history for the next 120 years.

Rediscovered in 1995, a replica was made and then given a make-over by local engineering students and placed here in 2009. The original is still at the bottom of the bay, where its remains are the subject of a conservation project.

By contrast, the U-boat on display at the U Boat Story exhibition (entrance fee included in the River Explorer Cruise ticket) is a revelation. Pride of the German fleet, the *U-534* was sunk after refusing to follow orders from Admiral Dönitz to surrender at the end of the war (a catastrophic decision which has never been explained). It was salvaged 50 years later and shipped to Birkenhead, 'over the water' from the British HQ for the Battle of the Atlantic (see page 32).

LOTTIE DOD

The only woman in history to hold British Tennis and Golf Championships

The Peerless Brewery
8 Pool Street, Birkenhead, CH41 3NL
www.peerlessbrewing.co.uk
Brewery shop: Mon–Fri 8.30am–4.30pm. Last Fri of the month 4.30pm–10.30pm and following Sat 12 noon–5pm
Merseyrail to Hamilton Square (or the ferry to Woodside). Take Cleveland Street off the square, then a 15-min walk to Pool Street (turn right for brewery)

S teve Briscoe's Peerless Brewery opens its tap room for 'Thirsty Friday' and 'Super Saturday' sessions at the end of every month, and Lottie Dod is usually to be found hanging around the bar as Steve has named an amber ale in her honour. 'We were stuffed for names for a new brew', explains Steve, 'when someone I didn't know mentioned a woman I'd never heard of.' Without hesitation, Wirral's (forgotten) Wonder was awarded this posthumous tribute.

In her day, Charlotte Dod was the female equivalent of Max Woosnam (see page 201). Born in 1871 at Egerton House in Lower Bebington (now a care home), Lottie enjoyed a life of privilege which left her free to pursue her obsession with sport. Apart from the advantages of wealth, archery (at which she excelled) was in the genes; a local legend has it that she and her siblings were direct descendants of Sir Anthony Dod of Edge, an English archer knighted by Henry V on the field of battle at Agincourt. No surprise then to discover that she took the Archery Silver medal at the 1908 Olympics while her brother walked off with the Gold. But this was the least of her talents: Lottie was a keen horse rider, mountaineer and hockey player who also mastered the golf course and the tennis court.

In 1887, at the age of 15, she became Wimbledon Ladies' Singles Champion, a title she was to hold four more times. She was the first woman to develop the underarm serve and to employ volley and smash as part of her game (the first woman to use the overarm serve was Tim Henman's great-grandma, Ellen Mary Stawell-Brown, at Wimbledon in 1901). Lottie also challenged the restrictive codes of dress that hampered the movement of female tennis players. She remains the youngest woman ever to win the Ladies' Singles at Wimbledon.

Lottie also became British Golf Champion in 1904, making her the only woman in history to hold British Tennis and Golf Championships. Not content with snoozing on her laurels, she played hockey to the highest level and represented England twice (in 1899 and 1900). Instead of a well-earned break when summer was over, she took up winter sports, riding a toboggan down the great Cresta Run in St Moritz, where she is also recorded as the second woman in history to pass the Men's Skating test – she was also pretty good at curling.

Disappointed to discover Lottie is not at the bar? Try her pseudonym: Skyline (that's a secret worth knowing).
Can't wait until the end of the month? Takeaway firkins can be purchased from the brewery shop.

WILFRED OWEN'S LAST LETTER HOME

'Dulce et Decorum Est'

The Wilfred Owen Story museum
34 Argyle Street, Birkenhead, CH41 6AE
07539 371925
www.wilfredowenstory.com
Tues–Fri 11am–2pm (call ahead to avoid disappointment)
Bus or Merseyrail to Hamilton Square

A 5-minute stroll through Hamilton Square Gardens (second only to London's Trafalgar Square in having the most Grade 1 Listed buildings in one place) brings you to the Wilfred Owen Story.

The museum only has one room, which is adequate for the artefacts on show but, as curator Janet Holmes says, 'There would be a lot more to see if Wilfred's brother hadn't flogged off so much of his brother's treasures to the University in Texas.'

Nevertheless, there is a fascinating exhibition commemorating wartime writers, such as A.A. Milne, C.S. Lewis and J.R.R. Tolkien, and another dedicated to First World War female poets including Agatha Christie ... also a rare BBC transcript of Siegfried Sassoon's 'Personal Appreciation' of his friend broadcast in 1948 and a copy of Owen's final letter home, finishing with these ominous words: 'There is no danger down here, or if any, it will be well over before you read these lines ... Of this I am certain, you could not be visited by a band of friends half so fine as surround me here.'

Owen was killed four days later (4 November 1918): the fateful telegram reached his parents on Armistice Day as the town bells pealed in celebration. A 'drawing-down of blinds' indeed.

All the Owen family's homes in town survive

The family's first home was at 7 Elm Grove in a relatively posh part of town. They then moved to a terraced house at 14 Willmer Road and finally to 51 Milton Road, a semi-detached in Higher Tranmere where they remained until 1907.

In 2013, Birkenhead 6th Form College named their new Humanities Building in the poet's honour – he would probably have appreciated the award more than the Military Cross he received posthumously.

If taking the train from Central station, don't forget to admire the mural fronting the Lyceum Post Office next door: this features the role of the Royal Mail in keeping families in touch during the biggest waste of life in the history of military conflict.

NEARBY

The Rathbone Gallery

When she's not looking after the Wilfred Owen Story museum, Janet Holmes runs the Rathbone Gallery at 28 Argyll Street (www.rathbonestudio.com): a small pottery workshop that offers classes as well as producing works for sale. This was once the home of Harold Rathbone's famous Della Robbia Pottery with a large kiln house around the corner now disguised as a Bier Keller.

There are regular talks here by Della Robbia expert Peter Hyland, who tells us: 'There was to be absolutely nothing which was mechanical and repetitive, no two pots were to be the same ... it is this spontaneity and distinctive mark of invention which is the basis of the charm of Birkenhead Della Robbia wares.'

The largest collection of the pottery's varied output can be seen on permanent display at the Williamson Art Gallery which, in 1928, was plonked 3 km away on the edge of Birkenhead Park – the first purpose-built public park in the world and the inspiration for New York City's Central Park.

WIRRAL TRANSPORT MUSEUM & HERITAGE TRAMWAY

30

The first passenger street tramway in Britain

1 Taylor Street, Birkenhead, CH41 1BG
0151 647 2128
wirraltransportmuseum.business.site
Weekends and Bank Holidays Mon 1pm–4.30 pm
Wirral schools' holidays Wed–Sun 1pm–4.30 pm
See website for special events
Arriva bus or Merseyrail to Hamilton Square station, then a 5-min walk
Ferry from Pier Head to Woodside, then hop on a tram (when running)

The Transport Museum in Birkenhead contains a unique collection of vintage trams, buses, cars and motor cycles and still runs a shuttle service to and from the Woodside Ferry Terminal thanks to a dedicated bunch of fanatics. 'You don't have to be mad to work here but it helps' is a common enough slogan found in dreary staffrooms up and down the country, but here it appears to be a condition of employment.

Since 2013, the museum has been run entirely by volunteers. Wirral Borough Council retains overall responsibility for the infrastructure and two of the trams, but the running of the museum, the maintenance of the trams and the driving are all down to the enthusiasts who devote their time to the place. 'We are all bonkers,' admits John Hewitt (operations manager), 'but we love it … we're as happy as pigs in muck.' A good job too, otherwise another feature of Merseyside's heritage would have disappeared for ever.

The service was started in 1860 by a man who made his fortune building railways and had a name to match: George Train had originally proposed a 'street railway' in Liverpool 'on the false idea that (the city) was progressive' but had been turned down flat. Across the water, however, he enlisted the support of 'the progressive and energetic' John Laird and, against fierce opposition from the omnibus operators, Train ran horse-drawn trams out to Birkenhead Park, Tranmere and Bebington. At 4d (4 old pennies) a journey, they were not cheap (six to eight horses per tram per day was a costly overhead) although cut-price 'workman's returns' made getting to work affordable.

Following electrification in 1900, fares came down and the tram became a more economical public service. To maintain social exclusion, however, the posher residents paid an extra 2d to be seated downstairs on First Class 'White Trams' which carried no demeaning advertising. In line with the gendered etiquette of the day, men tended to risk open-air travel on the upper deck while the ladies sheltered downstairs where signage on the wooden panelling reminded them that spitting was forbidden.

John and his crew maintain nine trams from across the world, including two from Hong Kong, one from Lisbon and three of the five surviving Liverpool trams. However, No. 20 (in service from 1901 to 1937) takes pride of place: rescued from a back garden near Chester, where it was pretending to be a summerhouse, it was restored in the 1990s using original photos and a new truck acquired from a derelict tram in Barcelona.

George Train: 'the best-known American on the face of the globe' and the inspiration for Jules Verne's Phileas Fogg

George Train was not born in Liverpool: he hardly spent any time here and when he put forward the business venture for which he gets a plaque on Lord Street (see opposite), it was rejected by Liverpool

Corporation. A financier, transport engineer, self-publicised globe-trotter, revolutionary republican, suffragist, anti-psychiatrist and jailbird, Train deserves wider recognition for his achievements.

Born in Boston in 1829 and orphaned at the age of 4, he was raised by strict Methodist grandparents who had an eye on a future in the ministry. Train had more exciting ideas, however, and embarked upon a career in business which took him across America (he founded the Union Pacific Railroad), through Europe and eventually Australia. His well-documented travels led to him becoming the inspiration for Jules Verne's character Phileas Fogg after he made a trip around the world in 80 days ... despite a two-week break in a French jail for supporting the Communards in Paris.

In 1860, Train opened an office at 23 Lord Street and spent the best part of the American Civil War here, trying to set up a tramway company and criticising the Confederacy. Liverpool was not happy with his politics or his trams, which ran on rails set hazardously above street level, but he did get off the ground in Birkenhead and even in London after being arrested for 'breaking and injuring' a street!

Not content with making a fortune in shipping and railways (and the real estate the railways ran across), Train got involved in politics, standing as a US presidential candidate in 1872 and later as 'Dictator of the United States', addressing sell-out crowds around the country. He also claimed to have turned down the offer to become president of an Australian Republic. He was a member of the Thirteen Club (dedicated to opposing 'mediocrity, superstition, prejudice and pro-vincialism') and spent time in jail on obscenity charges for defending a female editor's coverage of an adulterous affair. He also financed *The Revolution* newspaper (in New York City) dedicated to women's rights.

'A sane man in a mad, mad world'

George Train became increasingly eccentric and was threatened with incarceration in a mental hospital. On his death in 1904, the Thirteen Club voted him 'a sane man in a mad, mad world'.

The plaque commemorating this remarkable man can be found at 23 Lord Street, L2 9SA, but a shop assistant on her fag break told us that not only had she not heard of the guy, but had never even noticed the plaque on their shop front. A tram in the museum is named in his honour.

WARREN CREST

31

'He lived nightly, and drank daily,
And died playing the ukulele'

13 North Drive, New Brighton, CH45 0LZ
5-min walk from New Brighton station
Bus 410, then 10A from Woodside interchange, then a 5-min walk from Portland Street
By car, at the end of the A554 (off Albion Street)

W arren Crest is a rather stolid location for the birthplace of one of modern literature's most celebrated and dissolute writers. According to the B, D & M column of the *Liverpool Echo* (29 July 1909),

however, this was the spot, on the previous day, where 'to Mr and Mrs Arthur Lowry [was delivered] a son'.

The facts of Malcolm Lowry's origins are confused by some people's insistence that he came from Liverpool, which inspired so much in his writing. It is not helped by his brother's claim, in 1987, that the family home had been destroyed in the Blitz. Research by Colin Dilnot and the deeds for the house reveal that it still stands ... as does Inglewood, in Caldy, where the family moved a couple of years later. Lowry was a keen golfer in his early years, a member of Caldy Golf Club, and Hoylake Boys Champion in 1925.

As befits Warren Crest's suburban character, Arthur Lowry was a wealthy cotton broker – successful enough to see his son through private school and Cambridge University ... and to grant him a regular allowance, which he squandered on drink as he struggled to avoid the career mapped out for him. While still an undergraduate, the young Lowry wrote his first novel (*Ultramarine*) and an alternative future seemed assured. However, he was already on the road to full-blown alcoholism and, in a letter to Conrad Aitken at the age of 19, and with a gap year in the Americas behind him, he acknowledged: 'I have lived only nineteen years and all of them more or less badly.' Unfortunately, things were destined to get worse and Bill Peschel recalls him as 'one of the great drunks of literature, leaving behind a trail of broken promises, broken bottles and broken works'. However, among the debris emerged one of the greatest novels of the twentieth century. After several setbacks, Lowry produced a publishable version of *Under the Volcano* (acclaimed by Anthony Burgess as 'a Faustian masterpiece'). Success, however, only seemed to fuel his self-destructive impulse and within ten years he was all but forgotten. He died in poverty with copies of his masterpiece remaindered on the shelves of English bookshops.

Even in death, Lowry created havoc. The cause of death was variously described as accidental (choking on his own vomit), suicide (overdose) or murder (by his long-suffering and equally alcoholic wife). He penned his own epitaph (above), which did not make it to the headstone. The Bluecoat Arts Centre celebrates his genius every October in the Lowry Lounge.

THE STAR CHAMBER

32

Mockbeggar Hall

Leasowe Castle, Leasowe Road, CH46 3RF
0151 606 9191
leasowecastle.com
Merseyrail to Leasowe station, then a 10-min walk
Bus 423 from Sir Thomas Street
By car, take the Kingsway Tunnel and the A49/A554

Overlooking the shore at Leasowe and before you arrive at the Leasowe Lighthouse (see page 248), an ancient castle is still standing. Its lounge contains all that remains of the infamous Star Chamber: a court at the Palace of Westminster, named after the star-studded canopy depicted above the heads of those summonsed before it.

Originally established in 1487 to ensure that the landed gentry did not get above themselves, the Star Chamber was subverted by the Tudor and Stuart regimes to become a byword for corruption, intimidation and political repression. Closed in 1641, it was eventually demolished 200 years later, but the ceiling was salvaged and transported to Leasowe Castle.

The castle itself (or rather the octagonal tower at its heart) was constructed by the 5th Earl of Derby in 1593 to facilitate his interests in falconry and horse racing ... a stone carving of the Legs of Man discovered above the main entrance acts as a reminder of the Stanley family's rule as

'Kings of the Isle of Man' (1407–1735). By 1650, the castle had fallen into disrepair and it shows up on local maps as 'Mockbeggar Hall'. Its fortunes improved under Sir Edward Cust, who salvaged the Star Chamber ceiling and four tapestries for his library, adding oak panelling gleaned from the submerged forest offshore. He was also responsible for the 'Battle Staircase' in the entrance hall whose hand-painted nameplates commemorate famous engagements. It is claimed that William III spent the night here before embarking for Ireland in 1690.

An alabaster bas-relief on the first-floor landing repeats the local legend:

'From Berkinhevin unto Hilbre
A squirrel might leap from tree to tree.'

Which reminds us that in ancient times the Wirral peninsula was part of a forest stretching across the Mersey Bay and into the Irish Sea. Until recently, the petrified forest made occasional appearances (it even gets a mention in Lowry's *Under the Volcano*) and there are tales of an Iron Age port at Meols, a lost settlement and a submerged churchyard.

Lion, the first St Bernard to arrive in England (1815), was raised here by a Mrs Boode and painted by a precocious 13-year-old Edwin Landseer. Five years later, Lion and his son were immortalised in Landseer's famous painting, *Alpine Mastiffs Reanimating a Distressed Traveller*, which created the myth that St Bernards wander around the Alps with tiny barrels of brandy attached to their collars.

Wirral: the cradle of English horse racing and of the Epsom Derby

When Bert the bookmaker told his grandson that the Epsom Derby was originally run on the sands at Leasowe, he wasn't believed. After a lifetime in the game, however, Mike Elkerton discovered that not only was his grandad telling the truth, but this was only part of a much bigger story about Wirral as the cradle of English horse racing. OK, so I didn't get this from the horse's mouth but, as a well-respected racing correspondent, not-so-hot tipster and active campaigner to keep the Grand National at Aintree, Mike certainly comes a close second.

Racing at Leasowe dates back to 1593 and the arrival of Lord Strange (the 5th Earl of Derby, second in line to the throne and a patron of Shakespeare). He built Leasowe Castle's Octagonal Tower as the first grandstand in racing history. The Duke of Monmouth won the £60 purse here in 1682 before losing his head three years later.

In 1723, local gentry established the Wallasey Stakes with a prize of approximately 500 guineas (£10k at today's prices). Participants included the Dukes of Devonshire, Ancaster and Bridgewater, Lords Molyneux and Gower and Sir Richard Grosvenor. The horses were stabled at Jockey Lane (now Sandcliffe Road) and the race was run from the Black Horse pub (now Sheridan's) to Leasowe Castle and back. To be declared the winner, the first past the post had to 'win by a distance' (a phrase still in use today), i.e. 240 yards (219m). Fall short and the hapless nags faced a rerun: at 8km a heat, it's little wonder that the horses frequently dropped dead.

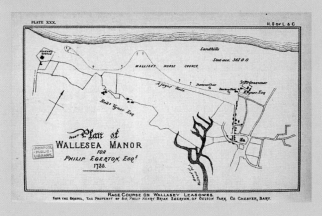

In 1732, encroachment by the sea meant that the Stakes were transferred to Newmarket and then, in 1780, to Epsom. Now 390km away, it seemed like time for a name change and, on the toss of a coin, Sir Charles Bunbury lost out to the 12th Earl of Derby and the 'Wallasey Stakes' were consigned to the dustbin of racing history. Nevertheless, Wirral maintained its status as 'the racing centre of England', with a total of 11 racetracks, the best-known being:

Hooton, until 1916, the home of the richest hurdle race in the UK;

Storeton, where Louis Napoleon rode his own nag in the steeplechase during the 1840s (the Lodge/Grandstand survives);

Hoylake, now home to the Royal Liverpool Golf Club (posts from the winning enclosure and the Jockey Bell still grace the clubhouse).

Nevertheless, apart from the odd relic and faded racing pages from the *Birkenhead News*, it is sad to report that barely a trace remains of the birthplace of 'the Sport of Kings'.

Apart from establishing regulated horse racing on proper tracks and inventing terminology still in use today, the Duke of Devonshire introduced racing colours at Wallasey before the Jockey Club took up the idea in 1762.

LEASOWE LIGHTHOUSE

The first brick-built lighthouse in Europe

Leasowe Common, Moreton, CH46 4TA
www.leasowelighthouse.com
1st & 3rd Sun of the month (12 noon–4pm) and during Heritage Open Days
Merseyrail to Moreton, then a 10-min walk
Bus 423 (takes forever -- best get the train)
By car, take the Kingsway Tunnel then the A59/A554, turning off the M53. Car park at the very end of Leasowe Road (past the castle)

A 130-step, cast-iron spiral staircase takes the stout-hearted visitor all the way to the top of the tower of Leasowe Lighthouse, from where views down to the Great Orme and the Isle of Man (on a clear day) are splendid. Breaks in the climb allow visitors to get a taste of life here for the families that maintained the lamp for 145 unbroken years. Anyone in search of a real secret might enjoy the photo of the submerged prehistoric forest. Taken in 1982, this was the last time the shifting sands gave up their long-lost treasure.

Lighthouses have been standing guard over the most treacherous stretches of Britain's coastline for centuries. The early ones were built of stone or wood (not a clever option considering the combustible nature of

the fuel used for heating the hearth and powering the lamp). The oldest lighthouse still standing in the UK (at Flamborough Head) was built – entirely of chalk – in 1669. Leasowe, however, is the first brick-built lighthouse in Europe. It was constructed in 1763 from handmade bricks manufactured at a nearby clay pit.

In conjunction with the 'Sea Light' at Bidston, the Leasowe beacon allowed approaching vessels to line up safe passage through the 'Horse Channel' until it was rendered redundant by dredging of the river and advances in radio communications. The lighthouse was decommissioned in 1908.

After decades of neglect, the derelict tower at Leasowe was rescued from its proposed future as a pub by a bunch of local campaigners. Starting work in 1989, the Friends of Leasowe Lighthouse began its restoration and had to shift six skip loads of bird muck before they could install the newly-forged staircase.

Child labour in 18th-century Britain

A child's fingerprints on one of the bricks in the wall of the Archive Room are a bleak reminder of the use of child labour in 18th-century Britain.

A woman's work is never done

In its 500-year history, London's Trinity House has never permitted a woman to take the role of Principal Keeper, but in the north-west it was a different story. The first female lighthouse keeper was appointed at the Point of Ayr in 1791, when Mrs Cormes was engaged by Chester, Liverpool Dock Committee followed suit in 1797, when Elizabeth Wilding succeeded her dead husband at Bidston; and, in 1854 at Leasowe, Ann Jones replaced her husband when he was dismissed for 'intoxication and insubordination'. The last lighthouse keeper here was Mary Williams, who ran the place with her eight children until it closed in 1908.

FLAG SIGNAL GATE

34

A colourful early-warning system

Bidston Lighthouse, Wilding Way, CH43 7RA
www.bidstonlighthouse.org.uk
Bus 437 from Union Court (Cook Street) to Upton Road, then a 10-min walk
Closest train station is Birkenhead North, then a 25-min uphill hike
By car, it is safer to use the instructions on the website as satnavs get confused

A concealed entrance and track lead to the lighthouse on Bidston Hill. Hidden behind it is a curious gate commissioned to celebrate the signal station that originally stood here – it incorporates authentic flag signals from the days before the telegraph.

At a height of 70 metres above sea level and clearly visible from Liverpool and Wales, the Bidston Lighthouse was ideally placed to identify approaching vessels long before they reached the mouth of the Mersey.

It was first used as an alarm station in preparation for the Spanish Armada and later during the Napoleonic Wars. In 1763, it became home to Liverpool Signal Station and alerted interested parties across the water (merchants, dock supervisors, families, brothel keepers, card sharps, etc) by providing details of imminent arrivals, using an ingenious system of flags. Over 100 of these 'lofty flagstaffs' ran across the brow of the hill and would identify the ship's owners, likely cargo and class of vessel (brig, man o' war, privateer, whaler, etc). A hole drilled into the rock to house one of these poles survives just to the north of the nearby windmill while charts on the wall of the lighthouse's lantern room decode the complicated early-warning system.

The first lighthouse was built here in 1771 as a navigational aid to indicate safe channels into the river. It housed the world's first parabolic reflector, developed at the signal station by Hutchinson (a privateer turned harbour master). With a diameter of 3.6 metres, it was the largest of its kind ever used. This gave it a range of 21 nautical miles and, at 3.8 km from Leasowe, makes it 'further from the body of water it lit than any other lighthouse, ever'. This system was eventually superseded, first by a semaphore telegraph and then an electronic one.

The lighthouse that stands here today replaced the octagonal one in 1873. Built of local stone to a design by Lyster, it provided family accommodation for three keepers in adjoining cottages and became 'Liverpool's principal lighthouse' until it ceased service in 1913.

Grade II Listed in 1989 but rarely open to the public, the lighthouse was bought in 2011 by Stephen and Mandy Pickles, who have devoted themselves to its restoration as a museum and offer regular tours supported by Stephen's encyclopaedic knowledge of all things maritime. If there's anything this man does not know about lighthouses, it's not worth bothering about. To discover the meanings of the flags, you will have to sign up for a tour (www.bidstonlighthouse.org.uk).

Bidston Observatory

In a maritime city, the importance of precise timekeeping cannot be overestimated. Sea captains would set their chronometers and merchants their hunter pocket watches from their daily GMT update via the observatory at Waterloo Dock. In 1867, the observatory was moved to Bidston Hill next to the lighthouse. To maintain timepiece precision, a surviving cannon from the Crimea was installed at Morpeth Dock and activated by a signal from Bidston Observatory at one o'clock every day. The original gun was capable of blowing out windowpanes on both sides on the river but now sits quietly outside the Maritime Museum. On a brick-built gun house at Morpeth Dock stands one of the three replacements: a reminder of days before the advent of radio communications. A silent movie by

British Pathé (www.britishpathe.com) commemorates its operation in 1932. Shame we can't hear what we've been missing since it was decommissioned in 1969.

Bidston Observatory is credited with 'a diversity of tasks of ground-breaking importance' but paramount were:

1. The calculation of exact GMT from its tracking of the heavens (it was said to be more accurate than Greenwich itself) from which the one o'clock gun would be fired; originally via a signal to the gunner but later automatically by electrical contact.

2. As the home of the Tidal Institute in 1929, it was in the forefront of developing tide-prediction machines under the auspices of Dr Doodson. It achieved 'national importance' in 1944, forecasting tides in advance of the D Day landings.

CARVING OF A SUN GODDESS

35

The Mani in the Moon

Tam O'Shanter Urban Farm
Boundary Road, Bidston, CH43 7PD
0151 653 9332
www.tamoshanterfarm.org.uk
All year apart from Xmas Day 9.30am–4.30pm. Free
Birkenhead North station, then a 20-min walk
Bus 437
By car, see map on website. Car park open 24/7
Also accessible from Bidston lighthouse

significant mortuary
terms. According to
and asymmetrical n
that distinguishes it
fragments that share(
50 km up-river, maki
those commemoratir
also has much in com
even be the work of t

Apart from its sym
factors that might ac
and personal meaning
According to Prof. W
unexpected ... West Ki
available skill within a
case that the relations|
person(s) was more im

Rather than being a
in the chain, WK4 m
'family project' undesei

For mure informatio
page spread.

West Kirby Museum
hearse-house to preser
Dawson Brown durii
between 1867 and 18
and include (Viking) c
a Man (possibly Green
pilgrims.

Armed with a 50p map of Bidston Hill, it is easy to plot your trek around this ancient site although getting lost is a distinct possibility. Among the well-marked focus points, the Lighthouse, Observatory and Windmill are standout attractions, but in the shadows, outcrops of soft sandstone have attracted graffiti artists for centuries: there is the usual stuff (initials of young lovers long since departed), the names of German POWs on what is alleged to be a U-boat and ancient carvings which have some sort of pagan significance.

The first of these is a life-size carving of a horse. Unfortunately, much of it has been eroded and is difficult to appreciate until you get the angle right. Experts differ over its date of creation, some claiming it as an ancient carving, others putting it as late as the 18th century.

The Moon God and Sun Goddess, on the other hand, have been identified as Norse or may even date back to the Roman occupation. The track to the Sun Goddess is easy to miss but once found she is remarkably clear: a female figure with outstretched arms and a symbol of the Sun at her feet. This could well be a Viking representation of Sunni, daughter of the giant Mundilfari (the Turner of Time). Sunni's daily task was to tow the Sun across the sky in her horse-drawn chariot.

According to legend and as surely as night follows day, as the Sun chariot disappears over the western horizon it is replaced by the Moon God, Mani, whose chariot is drawn by dogs although, as the God of walkers, he often sets a good example by striding across the night sky unaided. The morning dew is said to be sweat from a horse that accompanies him in his quest.

His carving is purported to be close by, but due to natural erosion and the interference of well-intentioned 'restorers', he is, despite his devotion to exercise, in less good health than his sister. For this reason, the carving has been covered with undergrowth and carries the following public health warning from the Friends of Bidston Hill: 'The carvings are extremely delicate. Please do not walk on them, clean them, outline them in chalk, or worst of all, attempt to restore them.'

Out of respect, we left the fading relic undisturbed and await its proper restoration in order to appreciate the full splendour of the Moon God.

HOGBAC

'A powerful st

St Bridget's Church, St
Mon–Fri 2.30–4.30pm
West Kirby Museum (
Merseyrail or bus 437 j
and through Ashton Pa

No longer in St
the church, thu
and reaffirming the

Known as West F
marker dating back t
bar motif, and the sk
housing, and has pla
interaction with nati
of the country.

WK4 has been g
of hogbacks stretchin
example, which has b
its execution. Some e:
masons who were out

However, Professo
imposed by Victoria

What have the Vikings ever done for us?

From Greenland to North Africa and from Newfoundland to the Middle East, the Vikings are in our language, our geography and our blood. Many Gaelic and English words are Nordic in origin (give, take, happy, muck, berserk, etc.), while Viking place names from centuries ago still endure ('Russia' derives from the name of Viking oarsmen, the 'Rus', who made their way up the Volga to the Caspian Sea). Meanwhile, ongoing archaeological and genetic research is showing evidence of widespread settlement and integration.

OK, in the process the Vikings got a bit of a bad press. The Anglo-Saxon Chronicle denounces them as 'a pirate host – plundering, looting and slaughtering everywhere' and they aren't recalled with much affection on Lindisfarne either.

Nevertheless, more recent analysis shows them to have been more than a bunch of marauding thugs; they were skilled artisans, ingenious navigators (getting to North America 500 years before Columbus didn't quite manage it) and shrewd wheeler-dealers who established an intercontinental business empire trading in silk, silver and slaves.

Still, it is hard to believe that, following his conversion to Christianity in ad 894, King Olaf had his henchmen wandering about Europe proclaiming that 'the meek shall inherit the Earth'.

But you don't need a pilgrimage to Oslo or to York's Jorvik Viking Centre to find the evidence: a trip to West Kirby is proof enough. Lying off the Irish Sea and overlooking the Dee Estuary, West Kirby played a major part in the lives of the Hiberno-Norse traders inhabiting this part of the Viking world.

According to Professor Steve Harding, the first Vikings settled here in ad 902 under the leadership of Ingimund and established their own Assembly at 'Thingwall'. Tranmere is Old Norse for 'a sandbank where herons pootle about' and West Kirby means 'village with a church'. In a recent DNA study, Prof. Harding discovered that up to 50% of the DNA of men from Wirral and West Lancashire is Scandinavian in origin.

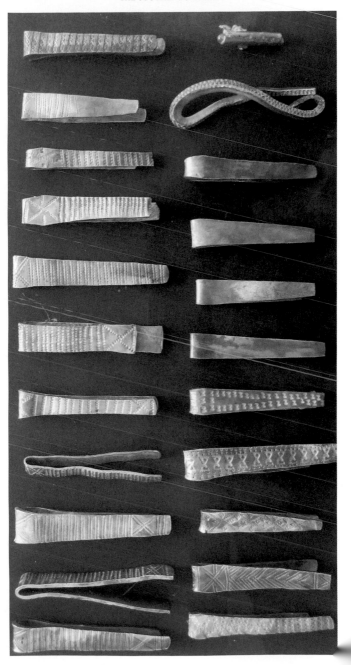

CHURCH OF ST MARY & ST HELEN ㊲

Pilgrim's progress

19 High Street, Neston, CH64 9TZ
www.nestonparishchurch.org
*For details of future Viking invasions of the Wirral, go to Steve's website www.
nottingham.ac.uk/-sczsteve/ or Karl's www.facebook.com/VikingChester/*
Merseyrail from Lime Street or Central station to Bidston, then the Arriva train
to Neston
Arriva bus 487 from Whitechapel
By car, take the Kingsway Tunnel and M53 to Jnct 4 and take B5151/B5136/B5135

According to early records, the Church of St Mary & St Helen (unique in the Anglican world for its joint dedication) gets its first mention around 1170, although the Domesday Book mentions Neston as having a priest in the previous century. However, fragments of Nordic crosses and grave markers discovered during restoration work indicate a Viking presence here as early as ad 930. Although the fragments were desecrated by post-Reformation zealots resentful of the pagan overtones, those that survive are well worth a visit. They include an unusual double-sided grave marker, the only Viking depiction of warriors on horseback and a brightly decorated replica of a complete cross inspired by educated guesswork. There is also a 13th-century tombstone depicting a Green Man being skewered by a Knight.

But there is more to the church than scraps of its Nordic past, and Peter Rossiter, the ex-churchwarden who is supposed to have retired but shows no sign of doing so, is proud to show it off. There are stunning sets of windows on all sides, including three designed by the Pre-Raphaelite Burne-Jones and one dedicated to naval hero John Monk, who fought in the Napoleonic War (1803–15) and was known locally as 'Nelson' on account of losing an eye and injuring his hand when fighting the same enemy. Original medieval tile work survives around the altar and a very rare stone Easter Sepulchre altar tomb is concealed within the wall of the Lady Chapel. According to Peter, most of these tombs were made of wood and destroyed during the Reformation – only three survive in the UK.

Finally (unless you want to go looking for the mouse carved into the woodwork of the high altar), there is a medieval  font famous for the fact that in 1765 Nelson's future mistress, Emma Hamilton, was baptised in it. Following the scandal of the age and Nelson's death, Emma was betrayed, imprisoned for debt and ended her days in Calais. An anvil memorial at Ness commemorated her birthplace and Dover Cottage in Parkgate is reputed to be her 1784 holiday home.

Vikings' pilgrimage

Local Vikings celebrate St Olaf's Day every year with two walks to places of pilgrimage. There is no shortage of possible destinations but they usually involve a church or two bearing testimony to Wirral's Nordic heritage. Beginning the day with a blessing at the site of the hogback stone in St Bridget's Church, we were reminded that Nordic tradition requires a pilgrim to shed one prejudice on the journey and replace it with a positive thought.

THE BRUNANBURH VIKING

937 and All That

Poulton Hall
Bebington, Wirral, CH63 9LN
www.poultonhall.co.uk
Check the website for Open Days and tours
Merseyrail to Bromborough, then a 20-min walk
Bus 1, 2 or x8 from Sir Thomas Street to Bromborough, then a 20-min walk
By car, Jnct 4 on M53, take B5137 and 2nd right down Poulton Road

Hidden in a hedge in the gardens at Poulton Hall (home to the Lancelyn Green family for over 900 years), a metal bust of the Brunanburh Viking draws attention to the possibility that the estate, with its commanding view of the district, was the location of Bruna's Fort and commemorates one of the most significant battles in English history.

On the 18th green at Brackenwood Golf Course (where the greatest hazard nowadays is a touch of 'golfer's elbow'), it is hard to believe that this may be the site of the mother of all bloodbaths in the turf war between the Anglo-Saxons and the Vikings.

Somewhere on Bebington Heath in 937, the army of Athelstan took on the might of Anlaf's Norse invaders from Dublin and their Celtic allies in a battle for the future of England. After 200 years of bickering, bribery and bloody warfare, the Anglo-Saxons were hoping to rid themselves of the Dane once and for all ... the battle is placed on Merseyside for several reasons.

A poem in the *Anglo-Saxon Chronicle* names Brunanburh (meaning Bruna's Fort) as the battle site (until the 18th century, Bromborough enjoyed the Norse spelling). The Wirral peninsula had become 'a well-established community of Norse settlers ... sympathetic to any military Norse expedition entering or leaving by either estuary'. With the Dee on the Irish Sea, this was the most logical landfall for any invading force from Dublin. In the event of defeat, a quick getaway was assured.

The poem makes clear that Anlaf made his escape to Dublin from 'Dingesmere', which Stephen Harding has identified as 'the wetland' controlled by the Norse Assembly at Thingwall: 'In no other locality does the context of geography, politics and place-names accord so well with the few facts we possess concerning the battle ... if Brunanburh is Bromborough, there is little doubt that it was on the ridge from Spital to Higher Bebington that the battle was fought.'

A war of words continues to rage regarding the true site of the battle. In the absence of anything but circumstantial evidence, there are 40 claims to the scene of the 'Great Battle', including Devon, Dumfries and – according to TV historian Michael Wood – a lay-by on the A1 somewhere near Doncaster.

Should you be lucky enough to join a tour of Poulton Hall, look out for the attic room converted into a replica of 221b Baker Street by Richard Lancelyn Green, leading scholar of Sherlock Holmes and biographer of Arthur Conan Doyle.

A 'must-see' reminder of the age of the steam train

Hadlow Road, Willaston, CH64 2UQ
willastoninwirralresidents.org/friends-of-hadlow-road-station-2
*Merseyrail to Hooton, then walk or cycle 2.4 km via the Wirral Way (concealed
entrance on the left just over the railway bridge)*
*By car, take M53 to Jnct 4, then follow the A5137/B5136/B5151 to Willaston.
Hadlow Road is clearly marked opposite the Nag's Head*

For those rail buffs too young to recall the age of the steam train, Hadlow Road Station is a 'must-see' reminder of the days when even the tiniest hamlet was served by the railway.

Lovingly restored to their 1950s glory, the stationmaster's house, waiting room, booking office and signal box are decked out in traditional livery and adorned with distinctive maroon signage from the days of British Rail. The ticket office window doubles as a portal into this bygone age with its very own Skimbleshanks snoozing on the stationmaster's chair, oblivious to the man's breakfast cooling on the desktop. Dotted around the office are working timetables, adverts and the odd 10-bob note: you can almost catch the sooty whiff of the 11.39 as it disappears into the night.

The station is a tangible reminder of the branch line that opened

in 1886 and linked the colliery at Parkgate (see page 262) to the BJR connection at Hooton. An extension to West Kirby enabled onward travel to Chester and Liverpool and, via New Brighton, to Euston. At its peak, Hadlow Road handled 40 passenger trains per day and survived the closure of the colliery in 1927. In 1956, however, BR closed the passenger service and in 1962 the last goods train stopped at all of the former passenger stations and any remaining fixtures and fittings of value were removed. The 20-km track was taken away to form the Wirral Way, a footpath, bridleway and cycle track running through the country's first designated Country Park. The station was restored as one of two visitor centres on the route and, since 2014, has been maintained by the Friends of Hadlow Road Station.

Until the 1960s, stations such as this were the lifeblood of rural communities across the country, but the fate of Hadlow Road foreshadowed the demise of many of the others. In 1962, Dr Beeching, a trained physicist with the heart of an accountant, was hired by the Minister of Transport (a road builder) to axe 30% of branch lines across Britain.

Fresh milk is no longer delivered by rail and the porter got his P45 yonks ago, but at least Hadlow Road still has its cat.

ACKNOWLEDGEMENTS

Special thanks to Sue Bone, Jana Gough, Joseph Sharples (Liverpool: Pevsner City Guide), David Hearn (www.liverpoolheritage.co.uk), Frank Milner, Gerry Corden (gerryco23.wordpress.com), Leonie Sedman, Stephen Harding, Richie Baker (richietheranger@gmail.com), Clem Fisher, Catherine Marcangeli, Steve Shepherd, Annette Butler, Chris Hampshire, Dan Rix, Gavin Davenport, Bryan Biggs, Greg Quiery, Jane Barrett, John Dempsey, Kate Martinez, Kimberley Tung, Maggie Williams, George Hawkins, Mary Colston, Mike Chitty, Mike Elkerton, Pat Laycock, John Reppion, Mike Faulkner, Nick Willasey, Patrick Neill, Peter Rossiter, Phil Waldron, Reg Yorke, Robert Cole, Robert Lee, Roger O'Hara, Roger Hull, Ron Cowell, Joe Byrne, Poppy Learman, Andy Edwards, Graham Jones, Olwen McLaughlin, Andy Povey, Fiona and Dominic Hornsby, Chris Iles, Peter Goodhew, Adrienne Mayers, Rita Smith, Rabindra and Amrit Singh, Tom Murphy, Pauline Fielding, Helen Moslin, Tony Crowley, Frank Cain, John Halliday, Mark Blundell, Robert Mount, Mike Dow, Gladys Rimmer-Armstrong, Fran Carlton, Rupert Hale, Gill Hoffs, Steve Briscoe, Janet Holmes, John Hewitt, Mandy and Stephen Pickles, Scirard Lancelyn-Green.

PHOTOGRAPHY CREDITS

All photographs by **Mike Keating** except

Quarantine Bible - Image courtesy of Border Force National Museum.

Ink drawing of Percy Galkoff by Sophie Herxheimer for Museum of Liverpool, reproduced by kind permission of the artist.

Nocturne to the City by Maurice Cockrill reproduced with kind permission of the artist's estate. Image courtesy of Victoria Gallery and Museum.

Cigarette cards of Everton Toffee Lady and Max Woosnam reprinted with permission of Imperial Tobacco Ltd.

Photograph of Frank Soo reproduced with kind permission of Roger Walsh – Club Historian Luton Town FC.

Liverpool 800 image copyright The Singh Twins:www.singhtwins.co.uk.

Photo of Sefton Suite reproduced with permission of Britannia Hotels.

Photo of Smit painting of the Liverpool Pigeon reproduced with permission of National Museums Liverpool.

Line drawing of John Hulley courtesy of Ray Hulley www.johnhulley-olympics.co.uk/

Eruption of the Soufrière Mountains by Turner reproduced with permission of Victoria Gallery and Museum.

Photo of the Brass porthole of the RMS Tayleur courtesy of Warrington Museum & Art Gallery (Culture Warrington).

Lottie Dod portrait reproduced with kind permission of Steve Briscoe www.peerlessbrewing.co.uk

Plate of Crown Street station reproduced courtesy of Liverpool Record Office, Liverpool Libraries.

Map of Wallesea Manor reprinted from an article published by the Journal of the Historic Society of Lancashire and Cheshire in 1893.

Cartography: Cyrille Suss — **Design:** Emmanuelle Willard Toulemonde — **Editing:** Jana Gough — **Proofreading:** Kimberly Bess — **Publishing:** Clémence Mathé

© JONGLEZ 2020

Registration of copyright: January 2020 – Edition: 01b

ISBN: 978-2-36195-324-9

Printed in Bulgaria by Multiprint

FROM THE SAME PUBLISHER

PHOTO BOOKS

Abandoned America
Abandoned Australia
Abandoned Asylums
Abandoned France
Abandoned Italy
Abandoned Japan
After the Final Curtain - The Fall of the American Movie Theater
After the FInal Curtain - America's Abandoned Theaters
Baikonur - Vestiges of the Soviet space programme
Chernobyl's Atomic Legacy
Forbidden Places - Exploring our Abandoned Heritage Vol. 1
Forbidden Places - Exploring our Abandoned Heritage Vol. 2
Forbidden Places - Exploring our Abandoned Heritage Vol. 3
Forgotten Heritage
Private Islands for Rent
Unusual Hotels - Europe
Unusual Hotels - France
Unusual Hotels of the World
Unusual Hotels - UK & Ireland

'SECRET' GUIDES

New York Hidden bars & restaurants
Secret Amsterdam
Secret Bali - An unusual guide
Secret Barcelona
Secret bars & restaurants in Paris
Secret Belfast
Secret Brighton - An unusual guide
Secret Brooklyn
Secret Brussels
Secret Buenos Aires
Secret Campania
Secret Cape Town
Secret Copenhagen
Secret Dublin   An unusual guide
Secret Edinburgh - An unusual guide
Secret Florence
Secret French Riviera
Secret Geneva
Secret Granada
Secret Helsinki
Secret Istanbul
Secret Lisbon
Secret London - An unusual guide

Secret London - Unusual bars & restaurants
Secret Madrid
Secret Mexico City
Secret Milan
Secret Montreal - An unusual guide
Secret Naples
Secret New Orleans
Secret New York - An unusual guide
Secret New York - Curious activities
Secret Prague
Secret Provence
Secret Rio
Secret Rome
Secret Tokyo
Secret Tuscany
Secret Venice
Secret Vienna
Secret Washington D.C.
Unusual Nights in Paris
Unusual Shopping in Paris
Unusual Wines

'SOUL OF' GUIDES

Soul of Lisbon - A guide to 30 exceptional experiences
Soul of Los Angeles - A guide to 30 exceptional experiences
Soul of Tokyo - A guide to 30 exceptional experiences

Follow us on Facebook, Instagram and Twitter

Thomas Jonglez

It was September 1995 and Thomas Jonglez was in Peshawar, the northern Pakistani city 20 kilometres from the tribal zone he was to visit a few days later. It occurred to him that he should record the hidden aspects of his native city, Paris, which he knew so well. During his seven-month trip back home from Beijing, the countries he crossed took in Tibet (entering clandestinely, hidden under blankets in an overnight bus), Iran and Kurdistan. He never took a plane but travelled by boat, train or bus, hitchhiking, cycling, on horseback or on foot, reaching Paris just in time to celebrate Christmas with the family.

On his return, he spent two fantastic years wandering the streets of the capital to gather material for his first "secret guide", written with a friend. For the next seven years he worked in the steel industry until the passion for discovery overtook him. He launched Jonglez Publishing in 2003 and moved to Venice three years later.

In 2013, in search of new adventures, the family left Venice and spent six months travelling to Brazil, via North Korea, Micronesia, the Solomon Islands, Easter Island, Peru and Bolivia. After seven years in Rio de Janeiro, he now lives in Berlin with his wife and three children. Jonglez Publishing produces a range of titles in nine languages, released in 30 countries.